# The Power of Identity

CHATHAM HOUSE STUDIES IN POLITICAL THINKING
SERIES EDITOR: George J. Graham Jr.
*Vanderbilt University*

# THE POWER OF IDENTITY
## Politics in a New Key

Kenneth R. Hoover
*Western Washington University*

with

James Marcia
*Simon Fraser University*

and

Kristen Parris
*Western Washington University*

CHATHAM HOUSE PUBLISHERS, INC.
Chatham, New Jersey

*The Power of Identity: Politics in a New Key*
Chatham House Publishers, Inc.
Post Office Box One
Chatham, New Jersey 07928

Publisher: Edward Artinian
Cover design: Lawrence Ratzkin
Production supervisor: Katharine Miller
Composition: Bang, Motley, Olufsen
Printing and binding: R.R. Donnelley and Sons Company

LIBRARY OF CONGRESS CATALOGING-IN-PUBLICATION DATA

Hoover, Kenneth R., 1940–
    The power of identity: politics in a new key / Kenneth R.
Hoover with James Marcia and Kristen Parris.
        p.   cm. — (Chatham house studies in political thinking)
    Includes bibliographical references (p. ) and index.
    ISBN 1-56643-051-8
    1. Group identity—Political aspects. 2. Identity (Psychology)
—Political aspects. 3. Political psychology. 4. Political
sociology.   I. Marcia, J.E. (James E.)   II. Parris, Kristen Diane,
1955–  .   III. Title.   IV. Series.
JA74.5.H66    1997
320'.01'9—dc21                                             96-51258
                                                                CIP

To Robb Lee Hoover
*brother, mentor, friend*

# Contents

# Contents

# Preface

Identity has interesting origins as a concept. The guiding research on the formation of identity was done in the 1940s, 1950s, and 1960s amid swirling currents of history, politics, and culture. Beginning in the 1970s, these formulations were tested in a stream of empirical research that today allows us to have a much surer sense of the meaning of identity for politics. The knowledge is sufficiently settled that it is time to interpret and summarize what has been learned.

My history with this inquiry very nearly brackets the period from the years when identity first began to interest political scientists down to the present time, when identity has become a principal political concept. Beginning with a doctoral dissertation in political science at the University of Wisconsin advised by Murray Edelman, this research was first reported in a 1975 book, *A Politics of Identity*. While that work is an important source for the present effort, the emphasis of this book is on what has happened since—both to our understanding of identity and, as a consequence, to normative thinking about politics. Scholars of politics were not much interested in identity twenty years ago; today the concept is at the center of political inquiry.

A book that undertakes a subject as large as identity and its relation to politics necessarily draws on a wide variety of influences and sources. I wish to acknowledge the valuable suggestions and comments on earlier formulations of these arguments from Fred Dallmayr, Notre Dame; James Davies, University of Oregon; Christine DiStefano, University of Washington; Donald Emmerson, University of Wisconsin; George Graham Jr., Vanderbilt University; Preston King, Lancaster University; Ali Mazrui, Binghamton University–SUNY; Raymond Plant, St. Catherine's College, Oxford; and Paul Thomas, University of California–Berkeley. Colleagues from several disciplines at Western Washington University gave me the benefit of their thinking: Don Alper, Vernon Johnson, Ralph Miner, and Debra Salazar in political science; Lena Eriksen and Ronald Kleinknecht in psychology, and especially Dana Jack of Fairhaven College and Carl Simpson, sociology. I hope they will find the results worthy of their effort even where I may differ from their views.

Two other particularly helpful colleagues are represented here directly. As a way of summarizing social psychological research on identity, I have reprinted a chapter by James Marcia, professor of psychology at Simon Fraser University, in which he summarizes twenty-five years of "identity status" research. To illustrate the uses that can be made of identity analysis, an insightful discussion of political change in a Chinese community, written by Kristen Parris, associate professor of political science at Western Washington University, is also included. These two essays make up part two of this book.

Other influences on this text are observations, and some minor participation, in political changes that have both challenged my ideas and focused my work. Explorations as academician and tourist in Europe, Asia, Africa, and North America have provided new arenas for testing ideas and witnessing the phenomena of politics and of identity. Colleagues on the Research Committee on Political Philosophy of the International Political Science Association have been particularly valued companions on these journeys. The result, as I hope the reader will find, is an interpretation of what has been learned about identity from the field of psychology in a form directly applicable to the classic questions of politics.

Finally, I must express my gratitude to Western Washington University, to the dean of the College of Arts and Sciences, Peter Elich, and to Geri Walker of the Bureau for Faculty Research, who, along with my colleagues in the social sciences, have made this a productive and stimulating place to work. Assistance from Emily Stordahl, Maaren Sanderson, and Marge Backman has lightened the burden of this work. My wife, Judith

Maybee Hoover, shared her experience of politics, her wisdom about identity, and her love, in making this book possible.

As Hannah Pitkin suggested in *Fortune Is a Woman*, the purpose of political theory, as opposed to philosophy, is to distinguish what can be changed from what is unchanging in the human condition. An understanding of identity does, I believe, provide the means of making that critical distinction. So, with apologies to Suzanne K. Langer, who wrote a most influential book, *Philosophy in a New Key*, I have suggested in the subtitle that we must come to hear what we know about politics "in a new key."

Comments from readers are most welcome: I may be reached on the Internet at *khoover@henson.cc.wwu.edu.*

I think that one's sense of identity should not be restricted to what one could not deny if questioned by a bigot of whatever denomination. It should be based on what one can assert as a positive core, an active mutuality, a real community. This would force fewer people to become (because they try too hard not to become) radical and religious caricatures. It would also force new standards on communities: do they or do they not provide a positive, a non-neurotic, sense of identity?

... [people] on this earth owe each other something like what I call identity.

— Erik Erikson

# PART ONE

# Identity,
# Power,
# and Authority

# I

# Why Identity?

Who are you? If asked that question, most of us would say something like: "I work at the mall, my family lives in Pough-keepsie, and I go to the Baptist church." As an afterthought, you might mention that you are a Republican and a member of the National Rifle Association. We all have an answer to that question, or, if we do not, we are in some sort of trouble.

The trouble in not knowing who we are consists of confusion within, as well as suspicion without. If the confusion within is bad enough, it is called an "identity crisis"—something worse than the flu, but not expected to be fatal. If someone cannot place us in a frame of reference, he or she may say, as they do in the old cowboy movies with a hand resting on a holster, "You're a stranger 'round these parts, aren't you?"

After a decade of wars involving ethnic cleansing, of turf struggles among rival gangs, and of contests over marital role structures, we know that people will fight to assert or protect who they are as readily as they will to save their standard of living or their property rights. Identity can be banal—the interesting person at the party is usually the one who is a bit mysterious. It can be profound—that is why we worship rock stars or sports heroes and heroines or, at least at some points in history, great leaders.

People create whole nation-states just to make the point about who they are and how they are different from the people on the other side of the border. When Chairman Mao led his victorious revolutionary army to Tiananmen Gate in Beijing, he declared, "The Chinese people have stood up!" He meant that the foreign devils had been thrown out and that bowing to the masters of the old class system was over with. Mao represented a new, plain-clothes Chinese identity. Just as surely, Mahatma Gandhi, spinning cotton in his ashram dressed only in a loincloth, established a focal point for the mobilization of the masses of ordinary Indians against the viceroys of the British Empire.

Identity is pervasive and ubiquitous in politics. The politician who gets up on the stump never forgets to identify with the crowd and to commend them for who they are: "My friends, we are gathered here today to say we are proud to be southerners." If you are told your opinion does not matter, you might say, "Of course it does, I'm an American, and this is a free country!" And when political leaders have us go to war, soldiers salute flags and sing patriotic songs—they do not balance their checkbooks or revise their résumés. For the Scots, the bagpipers who lead the charge remind them who they are right through the shooting.

In this book, we first see what identity has to do with political power and, on finding that a great deal of power flows from identity, try to determine just what identity is made of. Our investigation takes us into the stream of research that has been done on identity, not to solve every remaining question, but to locate major sources of insight and interpretation. This done, our attention returns to politics. How can politics be made to serve the healthier aspects of identity needs and avoid the pathologies that sometimes accompany the quest for identity?

## Identity and Systems of Power

At root, all systems of power involve an accommodation with human identity needs. Monarchs try to establish their legitimacy by serving as exemplars of national identity. As British royalty is currently learning, being an exemplar of identity can be the hardest part of the job of reigning. Totalitarianism is often rationalized through some collectivized concept of identity based in race, territory, or ideology.[1] Hitler's appeal was to the "master race"; Napoleon thought that he personified France.

4

Republics typically limit and stratify access to power to certain categories of people—categories that both reflect and establish differences in identity. Citizens are defined by excluding aliens and felons. Qualifications for office keep out the young and, in some infamous cases, women, nonwhites, and the propertyless. Citizenship is a marker of identity as well as a legal status, an entitlement to rights, and a set of obligations to legitimate powers and authorities.

Democracies are unique among systems of power in that different identities are dissolved, procedurally at least, into "the people." The logic of democracy is that citizenship should be defined broadly and should be available to all those who commit to the rules of a law-governed society. Identity as it relates to access to power is largely neutralized, though our own Constitution retains references to "natural-born citizens" in describing the qualifications for the presidency.

A defining characteristic of *non*democratic societies and situations is that entitlements to power, and even citizenship itself, are particular to certain identities. Aristocracies of birth or of class, race, or gender are commonplace in political systems. Sometimes these aristocracies of identity are formalized in constitutions and laws; at other times, they simply exist as custom and practice. Legitimation in nondemocratic polities depends on the validation of differences among classifications of people. Consequently, the task of changing nondemocratic societies depends directly on understanding the political dynamics of identity.

These brief illustrations are meant to suggest that identity is a highly consequential matter with heavy political overtones. One task of this book is to see what identity consists of exactly: how it can be distinguished from other concepts—race, ethnicity, gender, class, self-esteem, occupational status, and so on. This question leads to another: why is identity so important to people? And finally, how can we use a knowledge of the meaning of identity to construct a better politics or at least avoid the worst kinds of politics?

The politics we are discussing is not confined to governments; it includes any situation where differences of power, status, knowledge, or any other distinction compel people to engage in strategies of influence and persuasion that are the stuff of political behavior. While these distinctions may be sorted out according to levels of education, skill, or the command of force, for example, they have in common the fact that all of them are also sources of personal identity. Politics, in this broad view, encompasses the workplace and even the community.

What formal political systems do is to institutionalize procedures and policies that shape and manage identities so as to serve some concept of the common good, either procedurally or substantively. In the process of politics, identities are created, such as governor, legislator, or voter, that put in motion an interplay of roles that animates the making of public policy. The policies that get made apply to groups of people: welfare recipients, business people, polluters, or maybe everybody. Once again, identities are shaped or altered by these political actions.

Informal political systems are even more pervasive. These systems work their will on people's identities with tools as subtle as status symbols, or gestures of deference or dismissal, that demarcate the lesser from the greater, the honored from the stigmatized. In neighborhoods, at workplaces, and in networks of acquaintances, people engage in rituals of identity formation, maintenance, challenge, and change.

Understanding the dynamics of identity helps clarify some common themes in this bewildering variety of situations and circumstances. The power of understanding identity comes from being able to see the inner workings of every aspect of politics.

## Identity among Other Concepts

*Identity* has come into its own as a concept essential to the understanding of politics. Concepts such as *class* and *self-interest* that are associated with traditional ideologies may be declining in explanatory power along with the forms of analysis and, indeed, the political movements they have sponsored. Class-based rebellions, it seems, only replace one master class with another. Self-interest tells us many things, but not what has true value.

*Identity* now serves as a focal point in efforts to combine philosophical analysis with political understanding. We know that democracies are capable of hurting people as well as helping them, but that nondemocratic systems have a far higher potential for abuse. The challenge is to apply an analysis of the theory and practice of identity formation to the difficult problems of making democratic politics support human development. How can an understanding of identity aid in democratizing nondemocratic societies? How can this analysis be used to address the realities of sectarianism and exploitation that degrade and splinter many contemporary polities? The first step in undertaking this analysis is to specify the meaning of identity for politics.

The discussion of *identity politics* is a ubiquitous feature of contemporary cultural analysis. Identity politics has become an ideology in its own right centered on the struggle for political "voice" by marginalized groups in society. As an example, in Edward Sampson's presentation of identity politics in the academic journal *American Psychologist*, identity is defined simply as an artifact of power: "power ... involves control over the very terms by which the discourses about identity and subjectivity are held and persons' psychology developed; power involves the manner by which persons are given a location and a subjectivity as actors within discourse." Or, "the identities that drive identity politics are not in themselves unproblemmatical features possessed by individuals but rather are historically constructed, shifting political constructs that are as much to be distrusted as they are to be the focal point of various political movements."[2]

In this view of identity politics, identity seems to have no substance; it is whatever power makes of it. Identity becomes what, for political reasons, we, or someone more powerful than we are, wants it to be. In this reductionist form, identity is resolved into an issue of power.[3] While I share the premise that power and identity are intimately intertwined, and that identity is transactive in nature, that is not the same as simply translating identity into power. As research on identity formation shows, there is more to identity formation than assertions of power.

While the political purposes served by the ideology of identity politics may be admirable (or not), the reality is that, as often happens with ideology, the political movement has lost touch with the analytic meaning of its key concept. Just what *is* an identity? The analytic potential needs to be extricated from ideologies of identity.

While the reduction of identity to power has its pitfalls, so too does an essentialist position. To argue that identity *is* race, or *is* sex, is to engage in a curious political maneuver. If identity is *determined* by an unchangeable characteristic of the self, then we have the basis for arguments of separatism. If I *am* my race or my gender, then all those who do not share my essential characteristic are alien and separate. It becomes very difficult to confront racism and sexism on any terms other than force or numbers. It is to argue that identity precedes existence. Current struggles over "difference feminism" reflect a great ambivalence over the political implications of this kind of argument.[4]

To juxtapose the essentialist argument to the thesis that identity is *socially constructed* through customs and conditioning is to be confronted with a contradiction. It is obvious that aspects of gender *roles* and racial *stereotypes* are socially constructed for reasons having to do with power, among other considerations. The implication of this proposition is that these roles and stereotypes can be *de*constructed, as surely they can. But the question remains: what is left of identity when deconstruction has taken place? Is there some primordial human essence? Or is each individual, thus released from social constraint, free to assert whatever identity seems appealing? If this is so, we are back to the self-centered individualism of classical liberal political theory. While images of autonomy and self-sufficiency have great appeal, they do not fit with what we know about the social interdependence that characterizes human nature.

The purpose of exploring these implications is to suggest that concepts constructed out of abstractions have a way of imploding once the ideological infrastructure is revealed. The cure for this malady of intellectual life is to establish some sort of connection between concepts and observation. A great deal of observation seems to support the equation of identity with gender, race, and class. Common expressions such as "That's typical of middle-class white males!" encapsulate such observations even if they, perhaps unwittingly, legitimize such other observations as "That's just like a woman!" Establishing the truth value of these observations would require more precise operationalizations of gender and behavioral standards.

The essential problem is that the nature of identity as an observable social psychological process is rarely examined directly in the literature of identity politics. It does not even appear in current encyclopedias or dictionaries of political terms,[5] nor are historical studies of the term often cited in contemporary work.[6] Indeed, nearly all the contemporary works I have surveyed that use identity as a key concept either omit any discussion of the definition of the concept or proceed with a common-sense definition that does not reference any of the literature of identity formation.[7] The political uses of the phenomenon of identity are often discussed in detail, but not the research on identity as an attribute of human development. This suggests that political agendas are driving the discussion, rather than an inquiry into the dynamics of human development.

*Identity*, as it turns out, is a concept that seems to have become detached from its social scientific meaning. To understand how to apply this concept to build better politics, it is necessary to recapture the analytical meaning of the term. For that, we must turn to observations of behavior that tell us about how identities are formed—and de-formed. Having done that in chapter 2, we turn in chapter 3 to the pathologies of identity formation and the corruption of politics that follows from them. In chapter 4 the possibility of a politics that affirms the processes of human development is explored, and in chapter 5 we work out the relationships between identity, multiculturalism, and democracy. In the concluding chapter, the task of democratizing undemocratic societies and situations is addressed based on what has been learned about the dynamics of identity.

Throughout these chapters, the connections between identity and human development more broadly, and their meaning for multiculturalism and democracy, are seen to be vital to a larger discussion that has preoccupied twentieth-century political thought. The central struggle of the past hundred years of Western political thought has been to develop a conception of the human condition that can support a redefinition of politics

9

so that democracy becomes its central characteristic. This objective may be seen to have been approached from two directions: one group begins from the proposition that the human condition is characterized by some form of developmental pattern involving known needs, aspirations, and behaviors; and those in the other group take their stand with the uncertainty and open-endedness of human nature. The first we name the *developmentalists,* and the second, the *individualists.*

For the *individualists,* democracy is seen as a process for managing conflict over inevitable, and sometimes intractable, differences. Individualist conservatives, existentialists, deconstructionists, and the separatists and militants among theorists of race, class, and gender may be found in this camp. For the *developmentalists,* democracy becomes the means of finding, in the shared characteristics of human nature, underlying bases for agreement, conciliation, and the resolution of conflict. Here we may locate some varieties of communitarians, democratic socialists, and reform liberals.[8]

While this discussion has been taking place at the level of classic inquiries into human nature, a second level of political discussion has centered on governance itself. In contemporary political discussion, governance has become the synonym of coercion. Highly influential political theorists such as Friedrich Hayek and Michel Foucault have, for quite different reasons, focused on coercion as the essential aspect of government.[9]

The coercive view of government gives the individualists a reason to argue for the minimization of community power in the name of personal freedom of choice. Freedom and community are seen as opposites, rather than as interdependent. On this question, we would find Hayek and Foucault in agreement with the early John Stuart Mill and Adam Smith. Furthermore, a powerful critique of the political ambitions of developmentalists becomes possible: they are the progenitors of authoritarianism, the enemies of freedom, and ultimately the foes of democracy. Here the idea that people can act on shared understandings of human needs is seen to be a threat to freedom.

Nevertheless, it becomes steadily more apparent that in the absence of some conception of human development, and of the political structures and policies that can accommodate it, the polity of the individualists degenerates into unbounded self-seeking, enormous disparities of wealth and income, and even violence. While the market can order this struggle along principles of supply and demand, it cannot, by itself, produce sensible conditions for human growth and development. The polity of classical liberalism can adjudicate property disputes, but it cannot seem to address the great questions of the human and natural environment that hold the key to survival in the next century.

The purpose of this book is to illustrate a developmentalist approach to politics by focusing on the question of identity. At the same time, I suggest that governance is about more than coercion, and that in its voluntary dimensions there may be found the means of advancing a developmentalist program. I also suggest that governmental coercion plays a role in human development, most notably in protecting against the violation of developmental processes.

# Notes

1. See the discussion of the relationship between totalitarianism, democracy, and identity in the works of Claude Lefort and Martin Heidegger in Fred Dallmayr, "Postmetaphysics and Democracy," *Political Theory* 21, no. 1 (February 1993): 114–16, 118. The paradoxical point is that both totalitarian and democratic societies rest, in a sense, on a universalization of the question of identity. Perhaps that is the underlying link made manifest in the conversion of ostensibly democratic revolutions and reforms into totalitarian regimes in the USSR and Germany.

2. Edward E. Sampson, "Identity Politics: Challenges to Psychology's Understandings," *American Psychologist* 48, no. 12 (December 1993): 1223, 1219.

3. Sampson acknowledges this point in *Celebrating the Other: A Dialogic Account of Human Nature* (Boulder, Colo.: Westview, 1993), 65 n. 1.

4. Diana Coole, *Women in Political Theory: From Ancient Misogyny to Contemporary Feminism*, 2d ed. (Boulder, Colo.: Lynne Rienner, 1993), 198–221.

5. *Encyclopedia of Government and Politics*, ed. Mary Hawkesworth and Maurice Kogan (London: Routledge, 1992); and *The Black-*

*well Encyclopedia of Political Thought,* ed. David Miller, Janet Coleman, William Connolly, and Alan Ryan (London: Basil Blackwell, 1987).

6. Philip Gleason, "Identifying Identity: A Semantic History," *Journal of American History* 69 (1983): 910–31.

7. An exception is Anthony Appiah, who suggests the following: "... an identity is a coalescence of mutually responsive (if sometimes conflicting) modes of conduct, habits of thought, and patterns of evaluation; in short, a coherent kind of human social psychology...." Kwame Anthony Appiah, *In My Father's House: Africa in the Philosophy of Culture* (New York: Oxford University Press, 1992), 174. Or Cornel West, for whom identity consists of "the ways in which human beings have constructed their desire for recognition, association, and protection over time and in space and always in circumstances not of their own choosing." Cornel West, *Prophetic Reflections: Notes on Race and Power in America,* vol. 2, *Beyond Eurocentrism and Multiculturalism* (Monroe, Me.: Common Courage Press, 1993). While these are useful descriptive definitions, there is, as we later see, a more precise formulation available in the research literature on identity.

8. For further discussion of these distinctions, see Kenneth Hoover, *Ideology and Political Life,* 2d ed. (Belmont, Calif.: Wadsworth, 1994).

9. Cf. Friedrich Hayek, *The Road to Serfdom* (Chicago: University of Chicago Press, 1944); and Michel Foucault, *Discipline and Punish: The Birth of the Prison,* trans. Alan Sheridan (New York: Vintage, 1979).

## 2

# Identity Formation in Theory and Practice

## Identity Formation: Learning from Observation

Since nearly everyone has an answer to the question "Who am I?" it is tempting to think that everyone knows what an identity is. It is a little bit like having seen a few specific kinds of trees and assuming that, as a result, we know what makes one bit of vegetation a tree rather than a shrub or a bush.

For most people, not knowing what an identity is made of does not matter very much; for students of politics, however, it matters a great deal. If there is something at the heart of identity formation, and if that something has common elements among all people, then there is the basis for understanding and possibly resolving political conflicts over identity. If, in contrast, identities are somehow exclusive and inherent by the makeup of the individual, then politics must be concerned with irreducible differences and the conflicts that go with them.

To answer this question of what identity is made of, the obvious way to proceed is to take a look at how individuals form identities in real life. Systematic observation of the phenomenon of identity would require a very large program of research. One would need to include subjects of differing sexes, cultures, classes, and races. Individuals of varying ages should be studied to see if identity takes different forms and serves new purposes as life proceeds. It would improve the reliability of results to including the views of observers who have differing disciplinary perspectives. Finally, it would be important to develop a conception of identity that allows the researcher to see it when it is there and to know when it is missing—or damaged.

The dimensions of this research program roughly describe the life work of Erik Homburger Erikson, an interesting and unusual person.[1] We begin with Erikson, before considering some contemporary research on identity, because his work laid the foundation for the whole field of identity studies. We see how a clear-cut formulation of the concept emerged from a rich and varied lifetime of research and then how his concept of identity can be modified to incorporate new understandings arising from the latest research.

Erik Erikson had reason to be concerned about identity. He was born near Frankfurt, Germany, of an affair between his Danish mother and a man who was not her husband.[2] After his mother was divorced, he was raised in Germany by his mother and her second husband, Dr. Homburger, who had become Erik's pediatrician.

While traveling in Europe as an itinerant artist after completing his secondary education, Erikson was attracted to Vienna by its bohemian culture and intellectual atmosphere. Erikson came to be a part of Sigmund Freud's circle of colleagues and would-be analysts. He was taken on as a tutor to the children of Freud's patients and eventually was trained as an analyst largely by Sigmund Freud's daughter, Anna.

Identified as a Jew from his mother's heritage and his stepfather's name, Erik Homburger, as he was then known, became part of the migration of intellectuals and academicians from Austria and Germany to the United States in 1932. His was a life filled with challenges to identity—and with the possibility of creating a new identity, which he did, quite literally, when he was asked by the immigration authorities to state his name. In effect, he created his own last name: Erikson—Erik, the son of Erik. The name of his adoptive father, Homburger, was retained as a middle name.

On arriving in the United States, he was appointed to a position at the Harvard School of Medicine. Later, Erikson joined the faculty of the University of California, Berkeley. After experiencing a bitter controversy over a requirement that all faculty sign a loyalty oath to the U.S. government, he left to do research at the Austen Riggs Center in Stockbridge, Massachusetts. In 1957 he joined the faculty of Harvard University, from which he retired in 1970.

In the course of a life dedicated to generating systematic insights about human development, Erikson did research and clinical work with people, principally younger people, in cultures as various as those of the Sioux of the Great Plains, the Yurok of Northern California, the "normal" children undergoing a generational study at the University of California Institute of Child Welfare, the combatants and victims of World War II, the affluent and the distressed in Stockbridge, Massachusetts, and children, black and white, in New York City and in the South.[3] His European cultural background and his extensive study of Gandhi and of India's revolt against British rule provided additional sources of perspective.

His research yielded a series of books, beginning with *Childhood and Society* and including several more studies of the developmental patterns of the human life cycle. He illustrated the power of his theory through his biographical studies. He wrote a Pulitzer prize-winning biography of Gandhi and an account of the life of Martin Luther that became the model for an approach to biography called psychohistory.[4] Erik Erikson died in 1994 just as the United States, and much of the rest of the world, was being altered by the "politics of identity."

## The Foundations of Identity: Erikson's Theory of Human Development

To understand Erikson's conceptualization of the phenomenon of identity, it is necessary to see it in the context of developmental theory generally. Theories of human development typically deal with stages of growth and maturation. These stages center on turning points from infancy to childhood, and on to adolescence and adulthood. Sigmund Freud powerfully shaped developmental theory by pointing to the decisive influence of events in early childhood that mark the changes from the total dependency of the infant on parents to the manifestations of independent behavior that come with physical mobility and sexual maturation.

Erikson's great contribution is the addition of a "psychiatric theory of the psycho*social*" to the psycho*sexual* theory formulated by Sigmund Freud.[5] What Freud did was to trace the beginning of a theory of the stages of human development. Freud tied each stage to the physical, largely sexual, aspects of development. Thus the famous preoccupation with toilet training in psychoanalytic thought: it becomes the stage where restraint is introduced to the purely instinctive behavior of the child. Powerful psychological challenges are seen to result from this confrontation: the expansion of the power of the father and mother, the stress on the relational tie between the nurtured child and the now demanding parents, and the shame that results from "accidents." All this is grist for the mill of psychoanalysis.

Erikson added a second developmental dimension. While *physical* stages of development may set the agenda for psychological adaptation, *social* responses to each stage of development are likewise critically important. Erikson, like Anna Freud, was concerned with how social environments interact with psychological stages along the timeline of physical development. Social patterns of response, including arrangements of power, have a strong influence on the course of individual development. As Erikson summarized them, the assumptions are these:

(1) That the human personality in principle develops according to steps predetermined in the growing person's readiness to be driven toward, to be aware of, and to interact with, a widening social radius; and (2) that society, in principle, tends to be so constituted as to meet and invite this succession of potentialities for interaction and attempts to safeguard and to encourage the proper rate and the proper sequence of their unfolding. This is the "maintenance of the human world."[6]

While all this has a commonsensical quality, Erikson set out to chart the specific stages by which human beings move from stage to stage and to specify the psychological challenges faced at each stage. By matching internal developments with social responses, Erikson was able to identify eight stages in human development (see table 2.1), each expressed as a tension between pairs of developmental modes.[7]

TABLE 2.1

THE STRUCTURE OF HUMAN DEVELOPMENT

| Phases of physical maturation | Psychosocial developmental challenges | Cultural / political responses |
|---|---|---|
| Oral-sensory $\Rightarrow$ | Basic trust vs. mistrust $\Leftarrow$ | [Responses to |
| Muscular-anal | Autonomy vs. shame, doubt | each stage by parents, |
| Locomotor-genital | Initiative vs. guilt | peers, com- |
| Latency | Industry vs. inferiority | munities, |
| Puberty/adolescence | Identity vs. role confusion | institutions] |
| Young adulthood | Intimacy vs. isolation | |
| Adulthood | Generativity vs. stagnation | |
| Maturity | Ego integrity vs. despair | |

What anchors this developmental framework are the stages of *physical maturation.* The commonality of these physical stages, at least to each sex, gives Erikson's model its claim to universal application. Erikson began with the conventional sequence of categories for early childhood development (oral-sensory, muscular-anal, locomotor-genital, latency, adolescence) and added three more: young, middle, and late adulthood. Ages can be attached to each stage, but there is cultural variation involved, and the ages matter less than the natural sequence of the scheme.

The central element of Erikson's framework, expressed in the pairs listed in the table, are the *psychosocial developmental challenges* that arise as the ego attempts to reconcile physical changes and cultural forces encountered at each stage. These challenges to the psyche arise in the interface between life stages and social practices.

The final element of Erikson's framework consists of stage-specific *cultural/political responses.* These do indeed vary within and between cultures, as they must. Cultures must help individuals meet the specific challenges of their circumstances. A mix of practices, customs, and institutions may be found at each stage. His writings provide rich illustrations of the ingenious ways that cultures shape identities.

The universal element of Erikson's analysis is the physical pattern of human development; the particular elements are provided by the society's patterns of response and the ego's struggle to integrate these forces.

Erikson further observed that there was a cumulative aspect to development. The ability to achieve a sense of basic trust in one's surroundings, and to cope with episodes of mistrust, helps with the next stage: the development of a sense of autonomy and the strength to overcome feelings of shame and doubt. He terms this cumulative pattern *epigenetics.* The "identity" stage both draws on prior strengths and contributes, when resolved satisfactorily, to the ability to face subsequent challenges. For this reason, and because Erikson devoted much of his research to young adults, identity provided the pervasive theme that linked all the other stages in his epigenetic model (see appendix I for the complete chart).

Approaching the question of psychosocial development as a member of a "healing" profession, Erikson was drawn to the question of what contributes to strength as opposed to weakness in the process of development. By the logic of his views on the importance of social responses, he was interested in social —and political—arrangements that were conducive to strengthening people in their development.

Insofar as Freud dealt with the social or the political, it was in the context of forms of psychic expression or release from instinctual pressures. Erikson wanted to move beyond this reductionism at the empirical level and at the normative level.[8] As a clinician, he wanted to find curative strategies for his patients. As a sensitive citizen, and as a refugee from a society perverted by fascism, he was interested in identifying the cultural maladies that distort and degrade psychological development.[9]

Erikson was wary of notions involving the standardization of "mental health" for reasons that were based in his research on the variety of psychosocial practices that were adaptive to specific environments. Nevertheless, he saw in his clinical work sufficient patterns in the developmental "crises" of his patients that he was led to summarize them by means of polarities, as in identity vs. role confusion. He would hasten to point out that "role confusion" is not itself a weakness. Ambiguities about who one is may be inevitable; the problem arises from the inability of an ego to deal with these ambiguities effectively.

# The Making of Identity:
## *Competence* and *Integrity*

In the context of his theory of human development, Erikson defines "ego identity" as follows:

> the accrued experience of the ego's ability to integrate all identifications with the vicissitudes of the libido, with the aptitudes developed out of endowment, and with the opportunities offered in social roles. The sense of ego identity, then, is the accrued confidence that the inner sameness and continuity prepared in the past are matched by the sameness and continuity of one's meaning for others, as evidenced by the tangible promise of a "career."[10]

With this background, we can now approach these questions: What is identity made of? How is an identity created? What makes it durable; what threatens it?

Erikson's central proposition, generated from extensive clinical research, is that the common strand in human nature consists in a striving for identity based on two elements. The first is *competence* in productive, social, and personal relations. That is why, when asked who we are, most of us answer in terms of what we do—our vocations, avocations, and the statuses that attach to them.

The second identity element rests on a sense of *integrity* or integral-ity within a sensible world of meaning. So, when pressed a bit further about identity, we describe how we are fixed in the social firmament: as believers in a religion, partisans of an ideology, natives of a certain region, among other cultural and political possibilities. These affinities mark out the boundaries of the world we are integrated into.

Both competence and integrity involve transactions between the self and society. Competence must be both achieved by one's efforts and validated through social recognition. One cannot simply assert competence, there must be social recognition of some kind to secure the basis for this element of identity. No sooner is it said that "I am a poet," than comes the question, "So where is your published work?" Societies have myriad ways of both cultivating competence and certifying the recognition of it: educational systems, status hierarchies, licenses, regulations, ceremonies, to name a few.

Similarly, integrity is a state of mind, but it requires that there be a world of meaning that the psyche can make sense of.[11] Here is where systems of social meaning, such as religions, political loyalties, and ethnic ties, exert their influence. Thus identity is driven not simply by ego, or some abstracted sense of self, but by the imperative of achieving a sense of competence and integrity amid the promptings of physical changes and the interplay of powerful social forces.

These two aspects of identity, competence and integrity, form operational benchmarks for the analysis of human behavior, as well as norms for the evaluation of social and political processes.[12] By examining how individuals and societies interact in achieving and legitimating competence, as well as the available ways of integrating individual experience with social modes of meaning, we can begin to see how the phenomenon of identity works itself out in each distinctive setting. By observing the patterns in these interactions, we can begin to make generalizations about constructive and destructive developmental environments.

In view of the empirical validation of Erikson's concept of identity in more than 300 studies over the past twenty-five years (see chapter 7), we may have some confidence that this perspective will serve as a reliable starting point for understanding how political processes and policies can foster the development of identity.[13] These and other studies will find their way into subsequent chapters on the applications of identity analysis to the challenges of politics.

The connections between what we have so far learned about identity and the more familiar aspects of politics are now becoming apparent. The matter of competence obviously relates most directly to productive life, but it is also a considerable factor in the personal relations that constitute civil society and politics.[14] Similarly, a society's modes of meaning, or ways of making sense of the world, incorporate class, gender, race, ethnicity, religion, philosophy, ethics, and partisan affiliation, among other aspects.

Erikson's concept of identity specifies a motivation for the uses people make of the state, the market, and the civil society that illuminates nuances left out of analyses that depend essentially on distinctions between power, wealth, and solidarity to explain these three spheres of activity.[15] The state, the market, and civil society—all function as bestowers and certifiers of identity meanings in people's lives. There is, with this perspective, the possibility of a coherent explanation of at least some aspects of behavior across all fields of individual and social relations.

To summarize, identity formation is the name for "a process located in the core of the individual and yet also in the core of his communal culture, a process which establishes, in fact, the identity of those two identities." Identity grows and is nurtured or frustrated in a complex bonding of self and society. It is not simply asserted or assigned. It is the transactional nature of Erikson's formulation of identity, and indeed of his other life stages, that seems to elude most writers who seek either a stipulated definition of a philosophical variety or a scientific definition in the positivist vein.[16] The best of contemporary work on democracy makes this transaction a central focus.[17]

In consort with anthropologists and other social scientists, Erikson worked to establish the parameters of social response that might make it possible to achieve a sense of identity, as well as an avoidance of the pathologies of identity confusion. He realized that these social responses would have to vary according to the environment one was expected to live in. He invites other social scientists to take up the search for those forms of structure, ritual, and behavior that would be most conducive to humane patterns of development.[18]

Erikson means for this inquiry to be both constructive and critical. He calls for a political psychology that can, in the light of the Holocaust, clarify "the most devastatingly destructive trends in the seemingly most civilized and advanced representatives of the human species."[19] Clearly the path is open to the consideration of policies and forms of political and institutional action that would support a viable pattern of human development—and defend against the abuses of the process in the name of power seeking, exploitation, and mere utilitarian self-aggrandizement. There are, however, further developments in the conceptualization of identity that must be dealt with before these political implications can be addressed.

## Feminist Critiques of Erikson: Anatomy and Gender

Erikson's work was grounded in a lifetime of intensive clinical work with both genders in widely different settings and cultural surroundings. His work drew on the work of women scholars such as Anna Freud, Margaret Mead, and Ruth Benedict as well as male scholars, and much of his work was done collaboratively with men and women. More recently, feminist scholars have, in fact, paid close attention to Erikson's work, first as the target of a serious critique and then as a point of departure for major developments in feminist theorizing.

Feminist scholars have developed two major critiques of Erikson: his argument equates *anatomy* with *destiny*, and, alternatively, his work fails to differentiate gendered components in human development adequately. Of the substantive attacks on Erikson's usefulness as a guide to the good community, perhaps none has been so pervasive as that of feminists concerned about his seeming complicity in the "anatomy is destiny" argument.

The danger these critics see in his presumed biological determinism is the connection made from that viewpoint to an endorsement, implicit or otherwise, of inequality between genders.[20] Yet Erikson's point is that the influence of *soma*, while inescapable, exists in relation to psyche and the social: his claim is "anatomy, history, and personality are our combined destiny."[21] There are elements of choice in the two latter categories.

Rather than build feminism on the denial of anatomy and its influences, Erikson stands with those who believe that it is more empirically defensible to face up to the implications of anatomy for the psyche and develop identities that can cope with the dangers and incorporate the strengths found in each gender's somatic potential—a point made with respect to males as well as females. This point of view is consistent with feminist views that acknowledge anatomy without conceding inequality.[22]

Carol Gilligan, in her path-breaking work *In A Different Voice* (1982), takes a gender-specific approach to human development by citing research that points toward the modification and reconceptualization of Erikson's theory. She argues that the two genders are differentiated by modes of thinking as well as by variations in life crises and that this leads Erikson to misinterpret evidence about female behavior.[23]

The most significant of these misinterpretations, according to Gilligan, is that his eight stages of human development seem to place separation from others at the heart of the scheme in the form of Erikson's concept of "identity." Women are then viewed as aberrant, since their concerns for mutuality, caring, and attachment appear to be consistent through childhood into adulthood. Identity formation is defined as a problem for women, when in fact it is a problem created by a culture, and its theorists, who misunderstand female human development.[24] This, and her more substantive critique of Lawrence Kohlberg's "moral stages," allows Gilligan to embark on her own powerful analysis of the "different voice" of women.[25]

It is interesting that Gilligan's comments start from a willingness to consider that gender is indeed related to destiny through, as Erikson also thought, culture. She diverges from Erikson with her remark that throughout his concept of the life cycle, "development itself comes to be identified with separation, and attachments appear to be developmental impediments, as is repeatedly the case in women."[26] Gilligan does not abandon the term identity; she asserts instead that, for women, identity is a function of attachment and mutuality, rather than separation. Indeed, John Bowlby, in his work on "attachment" as a critical dimension of human development, suggests that mutuality is vital to both sexes.[27]

The concept of identity is perceived in this view as Erikson's way of endorsing separation and personal autonomy as a developmental ideal. Erikson has frequently been criticized for seeming to advance a simple model of individualism through his concept of identity. The similarity of this view to the principal assumptions of bourgeois liberalism opens Erikson to attack from its critics on the left and the right.[28]

Yet one cannot fully comprehend Erikson's work without understanding that his entire theory of identity is based in social mutuality. It was not attachment to the "other" that Erikson saw as an "impediment" to development—in fact, attachment is the essence of the process of maturation.[29] Nothing in Erikson can be taken to mean that identity is formed autonomously or separately, or even that individual distinctiveness is, or ought to be, independent of social validation. As he says of identity formation, "the process 'begins' somewhere in the first true 'meeting' of mother and baby as two persons who can touch and recognize each other, and it does not 'end' until a man's power of mutual affirmation wanes."[30]

The transactional nature of identity formation, as has already been illustrated, is the stuff of Erikson's whole theory. Since, in Gilligan's framework, separation is associated with male gender characteristics, the issue is critical in working through a model of development that takes account of both genders.

But Gilligan's more fundamental point remains. In Erikson's description of the "identity" stage, if not his fundamental conceptualization, he needed more explicitly to account for the social as well as the somatic differences that gender makes. Gilligan, Dana Jack, and others are making significant progress in this regard, most recently with studies of the loss of self-esteem in adolescent girls and in women deprived of meaningful relationships.[31] Even though Erikson's analysis of children's play constructions was gender differentiated, the epigenetic chart does not differentiate by gender. This needs to be done in a manner that captures the phenomena of identity and mutuality

24

in a gender-sensitive fashion. The most promising revision of Erikson's stage theory would fully incorporate, in the words of Carol Franz and Kathleen White, "the development of the individuated, socially connected personality" and "the attached, interpersonally connected, care-oriented personality" in both genders.[32]

This approach is consistent with the findings from systematic empirical research involving males and females. As A.S. Waterman reports, there is

> general comparability for males and females in the direction and timing of identity formation. The facts also support the observation by Archer (1985, 1989) that the task of identity formation is more complex for females than for males in that they endeavor to work out for themselves their goals, values, and beliefs in more domains than do males. Not only do females experience the desire to establish their sense of identity in vocational choice, religious beliefs, political ideology, and sex-role attitudes in the same manner as males, but they engage in more active reflection and decision-making regarding identity in a relational context than do their male counterparts.[33]

The point here is that women and men differ not in their drive toward identity but on the timing and the dimensions in which identity is sought. Both look for competence and integrity in many of the same places. But women are likely to work out issues of mutuality at an earlier time than men. For men, this component of identity is often deferred until vocational issues are nearer to being settled.

# The Making of Identity:
## *Mutuality*

Viewed from the perspective just described, the simple assertion of identity-as-gender is alternately too anatomically determined or overly shaped by culture, not cognizant of common elements in both genders, and likely to lead away from the peaceful resolution of differences. Gender is assuredly critical to identity, but to regard it as the exclusive determinant of identity is to deprive both genders of possibilities for the achievement of integrity, competence, and, it should now be added, a capacity for relational *mutuality* that contemporary research suggests is critical for all.[34]

Gilligan, Jack, Bowlby, Rubin, and others who have focused on developmental patterns in women contribute a clearer picture of the meaning of attachment, especially in the context of gender roles. While interpretations differ on the extent to which the sexes are inherently distinct, as opposed to culturally shaped, in their need for attachment, the significance of attachment for both sexes is much better understood in view of the research that has been done particularly on women.

## Operational Aspects of Identity: *Competence*, *Integrity*, and *Mutuality*

Consequently, it is important to add to *competence* and *integrity* an additional element of identity formation: *mutuality*. The attachments that make possible a sense of personal continuity are, independently of one's sense of competence, or of one's ability to integrate experience within a larger pattern of meaning, a critical factor in the shaping and maintenance of identity. This is true for both sexes. As Gilligan acknowledges, her work "indicates that the inclusion of women's experience brings to developmental understanding a new perspective on relationships that changes the basic constructs of interpretation. The concept of identity expands to include the experience of interconnection."[35]

The operational element here has to do with the ways that political and social arrangements support, or interfere with, the possibility of sustaining commitments to forms of attachment. Where intergenerational care is disrupted, where committed relationships are undermined by social practices, where abusive or exploitative personal behavior is endorsed by society, the formation of identity is endangered. The political significance of sustaining attachment becomes apparent in chapter 4.

With this addition, we now have in place a theory of identity that has three operational elements—competence, integrity, and mutuality—that can provide both observable evidence for the claims made in the name of identity theory, and conceptual foundations for a fresh analysis of political processes and public policy. It now becomes important to understand the dynamics of identity as they have an impact on politics.

# Notes

1. The most important of Erikson's works on identity are *Childhood and Society* (New York: Norton, 1950, 1963), *Identity: Youth and Crisis* (New York: Norton, 1968), *Dimensions of a New Identity* (New York: Norton, 1974), and *The Life Cycle Completed: A Review* (New York: Norton, 1982). On the relative significance of Erikson's contribution to formulating the concept of identity in its modern form, see the semantic history of the term in Philip Gleason, "Identifying Identity: A Semantic History," *Journal of American History* 69 (1983): 910–31. Cf. Kenneth Hoover, *A Politics of Identity: Liberation and the Natural Community* (Urbana: University of Illinois Press, 1975).

2. A fact publicly revealed only on his death in May 1994. There has also been some confusion over the Jewish element of Erikson's identity. His mother was of both Lutheran and Jewish ancestry; his adoptive father was Jewish. He never knew either his real father or his mother's first husband. Erikson stated that "Jewishness as such has not meant much to me," and he is reported to have become a Christian. One critic charged him with concealing the Jewish aspects of his identity, a charge that is hard to take seriously since he left Austria owing to the persecution of Jews, retained Homburger as his middle name, and referred in his autobiographical reflections specifically to the Jewish element of his ancestry. Cf. "Erik Erikson, 91, Psychoanalyst Who Reshaped Views of Human Growth, Dies," *New York Times*, 13 May 1994, B16; Marshall Berman, "Review of *Life History and the Historical Moment*," in *New York Times Book Review*, 30 March 1975, sec. 7, pp. 1–2, 22; Robert Coles, *Erik H. Erikson: The Growth of His Work* (Boston: Atlantic, Little Brown, 1970), 180–81.

3. Coles, *Erik H. Erikson*, 33, 43–44, 49.

4. Briefly stated, Erikson's psychohistorical method consisted of showing how leaders, having worked out developmental crises in their own lives, take on similar crises on behalf of their societies. Just as Luther dealt with the problem of rebelling against the authority of his father, so he became the leader of a people who were rebelling against the pope. Cf. Erik Erikson, *Young Man Luther* (New York: Norton, 1958); Erik Erikson, *Life History and the Historical Moment* (New York: Norton, 1975).

5. Erikson, *Life Cycle Completed*, 16.

6. Erikson, *Childhood*, 270.

7. For a full discussion of this model, see ibid. The *epigenetic chart* on which it is based appears as appendix A of this book.

8. Ibid., 7–18; Philip Rieff, *Freud: The Mind of the Moralist* (Garden City, N.Y.: Doubleday Anchor, 1961), 251.

9. Erikson commented to the author that his status as an immigrant to this country and his involvement in the loyalty oath controversy at the University of California made him somewhat shy of direct political involvement but that he retained a great interest in the political applications of his ideas. Cf. Coles, *Erik H. Erikson*, 156–58.

10. Erikson, *Childhood*, 261.

11. Ibid., 240, 268–69.

12. There is important independent empirical evidence for the behavioral significance of *competence* and *integrity* to be found in research on voter assessments of candidates. These two terms turn up as the key criteria by which voters evaluate presidential candidates. See Arthur Miller, Martin Wattenberg, and Oksana Malanchuk, "Schematic Assessments of Presidential Candidates," *American Political Science Review* 80, no. 2 (June 1986): 521–40. The authors find that these considerations are more important than *charisma, reliability,* and *personal characteristics.* Are our leaders evaluated according to our own concepts of idealized identities?

13. For an overview, see J.E. Marcia, A.S. Waterman, D.R. Matteson, S.L. Archer, and J.L. Orlofsky, *Ego Identity: A Handbook for Psychosocial Research* (New York: Springer Verlag, 1993).

14. Erik Erikson, *Identity and the Life Cycle: Selected Papers* (New York: International Universities Press, 1959), 48.

15. Jürgen Habermas, *Autonomy and Solidarity: Interviews with Jürgen Habermas,* rev. ed., ed. Peter Dews (New York: Verso, 1992).

16. Gleason argues that Erikson's concept is one-sided with respect to a somewhat different dichotomy, between identity as a principle of continuity and as an artifact of changing circumstances (cf. Gleason, "Identifying Identity," 918). But what Erikson refers to is the *search* for continuity both within the psyche and "outside" in the culture. The *reality* is, of course, that change is the rule both within and without, as Erikson's psychosexual stages and the psychosocial responses attest. In fact, the confrontation of continuity and change is what powers the whole epigenetic life cycle.

17. Cf. Benjamin Barber, *Strong Democracy: Participatory Politics for a New Age* (Berkeley: University of California Press, 1984); Jean Bethke Elshtain, *Public Man, Private Woman: Women in Social and Political Thought* (Princeton: Princeton University Press, 1981); Charles Taylor, *Sources of the Self: The Making of the Modern Identity* (Cambridge: Harvard University Press, 1989); and Iris Marion Young,

*Justice and the Politics of Difference* (Princeton: Princeton University Press, 1990).

18. Erikson, *Life Cycle Completed*, chap. 4.

19. Ibid., 23.

20. Paul Roazen, *Erik Erikson: The Power and Limits of a Vision* (New York: Free Press, 1976), 144–45.

21. Erikson, *Identity*, 285–86.

22. Erikson, *Childhood*, 404–5; cf. Elshtain, *Public Man, Private Woman*.

23. Carol Gilligan, *In a Different Voice: Psychological Theory and Women's Development* (Cambridge: Harvard University Press, 1982), 103–4, 154–55.

24. Ibid., 11–13.

25. Lawrence Kohlberg, *The Psychology of Moral Development: The Nature and Validity of Moral Stages* (San Francisco: Harper & Row, 1984). Cf. Nancy Hirschman, "Freedom, Recognition, and Obligation: A Feminist Approach to Political Theory," *American Political Science Review* 83 (1989): 1227–43; and Richard Sinopoli and Nancy Hirschman, "Feminism and Liberal Theory," *American Political Science Review* 85 (1991): 221–33.

26. Gilligan, *In a Different Voice*, 12.

27. John Bowlby, *Attachment* (New York: Basic Books, 1982).

28. Russell Jacoby, *Social Amnesia: A Critique of Contemporary Psychology from Adler to Laing* (Boston: Beacon Press, 1976); Joel Kovel, "Erik Erikson's Psycho-history," *Social Policy*, March/April 1974, 60–64; Frederick Crews, *Skeptical Engagements* (New York: Oxford University Press, 1986); David Gutmann, "Erik Erikson's America," *Commentary* 58 (September 1974): 60–64; Howard Kushner, "Adjustment and Pathology in Psychohistory: A Critique of the Erikson Model," *Psychocultural Review* 1 (Fall 1977): 493–506; Howard Kushner, "Americanization of the Ego," *Canadian Review of American Studies* 10, no. 1 (1979): 95–101; and Roazen, *Erik Erikson*.

29. Erikson, *Identity*, 265–67. Gilligan cites the same book for her assertion on this point, though without a page reference. Cf. James E. Marcia, "The Relational Roots of Identity," in *Discussions on Ego Identity*, ed. Jane Kroger (Hillsdale, N.J.: Lawrence Erlbaum Associates, 1993), 101–20.

30. Erikson, *Identity*, 23.

31. Carol Gilligan, "Mapping the Moral Domain: A Contribution of Women's Thinking to Psychology," Center for the Study of Gender, Education, and Human Development, Harvard Graduate School of Education, Harvard University Press, 1988; Dana Jack, *Silencing the Self: Women and Depression* (Cambridge: Harvard University Press, 1991).

32. The authors present their revision of the epigenetic chart along these lines. Carol Franz and Kathleen White, "Individuation and At-

tachment in Personality Development: Extending Erikson's Theory," *Journal of Personality* 53 (1985): 242–43, 248.

33. Alan S. Waterman, "Developmental Perspectives on Identity Formation," in Marcia et al., *Ego Identity*, 61–62. On the ways that differences in degree and timing of domain development create distinct problems and challenges for females as well as males, see D.R. Matteson, "Differences within and between Genders," in Marcia et al., *Ego Identity*, 98–99. Matteson concludes that future research will need instruments that go beyond the initial conceptualizations of identity derived from Erikson's work.

34. D. Bilsker, D. Schiedel, and J. Marcia, "Sex Differences in Identity Status," *Sex Roles* 18, nos. 3–4 (February 1988): 231–36.

35. Gilligan, *In a Different Voice*, 173.

# 3

# The Political Pathologies
# of Identity Formation

As are all life processes, human development is fraught with peril. The collective form of this peril is principally in the kinds of political regimes that emerge in consequence of structures of identity found in different societies. It was the attempt to build a regime on identity-as-race for the political purposes of fascism that drove Erikson, and millions of others who were identified as Jews, to emigrate from Austria and Germany in the 1930s. Politicized structures of identity have their great dangers.

The seeds of this collective peril are found in the reactions of individuals to developmental crises. Those who have tested Erikson's concept of identity have demonstrated the link between pathologies of identity formation and destructive political consequences. As we later see, either a social circumstance that forecloses the development of an authentic identity or an environment that precludes the maturation of identity in adulthood can contribute to authoritarian attitudes and exploitative behavior. Erikson has provided a conceptual roadmap for understanding the mechanisms behind these pathologies of attitude and behavior.

We consider, in turn, how negative identities are generated, why exploitation results from "pseudo speciation," what authoritarianism has to do with these pathologies, and where democracy can play a role in avoiding the worst effects of these phenomena.

# Exploitation, Pseudo Speciation, and Negative Identities

Exploitation succeeds by introducing denigration as a form of repression and backing it up with the use of force. Effective denigration requires the imposition of what Erikson identifies as *pseudo speciation*.[1] Erikson's definition of pseudo speciation and his analysis of the psychological consequences of exploitation are built on the idea that each stage of life has dual possibilities: *identity* vs. *role confusion, intimacy* vs. *isolation, integrity* vs. *despair*, and so on. He points out that

> exploitation exists where a divided function is misused by one of the partners involved in such a way that for the sake of his *pseudo* aggrandizement he deprives the other partner of whatever sense of identity he had achieved, of whatever integrity he had approached. The loss of mutuality which characterizes such exploitation eventually destroys the common function and the exploiter himself.[2]

The political aspect of pseudo speciation lies precisely in the necessity of using force to displace competency, integrity, and mutuality as a basis for human relations. The exploitation of women by men can be seen here as a manifestation of a generalized pathology of identity formation. The differences of the sexes become a readily available device of pseudo speciation and the attribution of superiority. Gender differentiation becomes sexism when it serves the false, or *pseudo*, developmental purpose of ignoring competence, violating the integrity of human development, and undermining the basis for mutually committed relationships, whether by men against women or the other way around.

Political structures can be used to reinforce pseudo speciation. Angela Davis points to the nexus between the legal penalties for educating slaves and literacy requirements for voters in the American South as an example of the overt manifestation of this approach.[3] Race was the basis for denying the education that would have allowed blacks to confront racial stereotypes through political means. Patricia Hill Collins illustrates how even the means of knowing about one's own identity can be subjugated though structures of knowledge that idealize one way of life at the expense of others. She reports that "the suppression of Black women's efforts for self-definition in traditional sites of knowledge production has led African-American women to use alternative sites such as music, literature, daily conversations, and everyday behavior as important locations for articulating the core themes of a Black feminist consciousness."[4]

Denigration as a form of domination reinforces inter-group aggression. As Erikson observes, "once we have learned to reduce 'the other'—any living human being in the wrong place, the wrong category, or the wrong uniform—to a dirty speck in our moral vision, and potentially a mere target in the sight of our (or our soldiery's) gun, we are on the way to violating man's essence, if not his very life."[5]

The specific form that pseudo speciation takes is the creation of *negative identities.* Erikson's analysis of the ways that the dominant culture creates negative identities for minorities was widely cited by leaders of the civil rights movement.[6]

Erikson also illustrated the point in his research on the Sioux. What was, in their culture, a highly developed system for bringing young people into a mature and self-sufficient adulthood was undermined by education schemes that caused the very kinds of negative behavior that became the basis for stereotyping Native Americans. Even the best-intentioned initiatives can go awry without a consideration of the dynamics of identity formation.

What makes these identity materials *negative* is that they are proffered by the dominant cultural group with a patronizing, even condemnatory attitude. The transaction serves to prop up the chauvinism of the master group. Sadly, its victims occasionally yield to the force of convention and accept the roles proffered so as to survive in a hostile environment.

For this reason, acquiescing to a stereotypical negative identity leads to self-hate. Erikson suggests that this feeling, which is often intensified in the identity crisis of youth, accounts for the more irrational manifestations of anarchic and radical attitudes.[7] In contrast, the success of one's positive identity generates feelings of self-mastery and ego gratification. The "black is beautiful" movement and the Native American "first peoples" movement capture the meaning of symbolic power over one's own cultural role structure.[8]

As Erikson comments, identity should not rest on how others adversely characterize one's makeup:

> I think that one's sense of identity should not be restricted to what one could not deny if questioned by a bigot of whatever denomination. It should be based on what one can assert as a positive core, an active mutuality, a real community. This would force ... a new standard on communities: do they or do they not provide a positive, a nonneurotic sense of identity?[9]

# Identity:
# Foreclosure, Diffusion, and Authoritarianism

We have, up to now, been focusing on identity *achievement*—a process, as James Marcia describes it, that has developmental advantages:

> Individuals who construct their identity, modifying or rejecting some conferred elements, also possess a sense of having participated in a self-initiated and self-directed process. They know not only who they are, they know how they became that, and that they had a hand in the becoming. Furthermore, they have developed skills useful in the adaptive process of further self-construction and self-definition.[10]

One aspect of this process of identity achievement is what Erikson labeled a *moratorium*. There is a period in late adolescence when experimentation and exploration permit the developmental latitude for the sort of constructive process just described. It is during such a moratorium that much of the synthesizing of past experience and future possibility occurs, along with the testing of negative and positive identities, and the reconciliation with pressures for choices of career and commitments to relations of mutuality. Although all these issues may not be settled at such an age, the developmental strengths acquired in the struggle play an essential role in the lifelong definition of identity.

The issue of identity may, however, be dealt with in other ways—and there are political risks involved. For many, and perhaps for most, identity is *conferred* rather than *achieved.* One's caretakers, perhaps in league with social pressures, present a finished identity to the young person. In the most definite mode, the process of identity formation is *foreclosed* either by circumstances or by the individual's own acceptance of what is offered. There is a sense of identity as a result, but it is not seated in the individual's own psychological maturation.

Finally, there may be a failure to achieve a sense of identity. The resulting identity *diffusion* becomes a troubling impediment as the individual confronts the subsequent challenge of *intimacy* vs. *isolation* and the remaining elements of the life cycle. Here the problem is that neither competence nor integrity nor mutuality seem to be within reach. The term *aimless* denotes the result for those suffering from identity diffusion. Serious identity diffusion needs to be distinguished from role confusion, which is an occasional problem for all individuals, and an identity moratorium, where vital processes are at work to make identity achievement possible.

Researchers have developed empirical means of separating identity achievement from identity moratorium, foreclosure, and diffusion—and have found highly consequential differences in the social and political attitudes associated with each resolution of the process. While the political dangers of pseudo speciation may be witnessed in "ethnic cleansing" campaigns and other manifestations of racism and sexism, the dangers of identity foreclosure and diffusion are manifested at deeper levels.

Empirical findings are clear on the authoritarian and stereotypical thinking that follows from premature identity foreclosure. As James Marcia reports in summarizing numerous studies:

One of the most consistent findings in identity status research has been that male and female Foreclosures, especially relative to Moratoriums, score highly on measures of authoritarianism and socially stereotypical thinking. They show preference for a strong leader over a democratic process, obedience over social protest, and the "pseudo speciation" described by Erikson: firm conviction that "their" group and "their" way are right.[11]

The same finding applies to those suffering from identity diffusion. And the reverse is true for those who are undergoing an identity moratorium in late adolescence, as developmental theory would suggest is appropriate.[12]

These behavioral correlates of identity pathology are affirmed in Erikson's observations. Erikson's illustration of the political pathology that can result from a fixation on authoritarianism at an early age was the Hitler youth. A preoccupation with gangs, violence, and totalistic forms of organization and belief are all, in this view, symptomatic of an unresolved process of identity formation.

## Tolerance and Democracy

Erikson realized that identity formation is not straightforward —there is a tension between positive and negative identities "composed of what he [the individual] has been shamed for, what he has been punished for, and what he feels guilty about: his failures in competency and goodness."[13] He concludes that "identity means an integration of all previous identifications and self-images, including the negative ones."[14] The schizophrenia of Dr. Jekyll and Mr. Hyde expresses the failure to integrate positive and negative identities.

Once again, Erikson's message is that perfection of the developmental process is rarely achieved but that the objective is to acquire needed sources of strength in dealing with the contested terrain between somatic development and social circumstances. Everyone is shadowed by negative identities that threaten and confuse daily life, but the key is to have the means of coping with, or even mastering, the urge to give in to the negative typing of oneself or others. The best countersuits lie in demonstrating competence, working out sensible ways of becoming integral in a community, and carrying through on a commitment to mutuality.

To sanction socially negative identities for African Americans and other minorities through legally enforced discrimination is to invite the confirmation of those identities in adult destructiveness.[15] Empirical research suggests that a strong sense of self-esteem can overcome negative stereotyping of one's ethnic identity. The question of redeeming ethnically distinct individuals from the pressures of culturally presented negative identities appears to turn on the achievement of competence, integrity, and mutuality by means that break through these stereotypes.[16] The bridges toward racial understanding that have been built by minority artists, athletes, writers, and leaders in other fields are evidence of how this works as a social process.

Identity formation is essentially a way of dealing with uncertainty and ambiguity. There is a paradox in Erikson's writing involving his observations on the impact of destroying indigenous groupings, such as Indian tribes, and his pleas for a universal identity. But the paradox is really a dialectic.[17] Unless individuals acquire strength from some source of cultural support, they will have a very hard time rising above the parochialities of a particular background to achieve a measure of tolerance.[18] To dismiss for anyone the importance of the particular context out of which his or her identity is formed is to enforce a kind of "homogenization" that ultimately makes identity all the more difficult to achieve.[19] This is the essential issue in the debate over Third World versus Western feminisms[20] and over the legitimacy of race as a foundation of identity.[21]

The essential link to politics is that effective identity formation is associated with tolerance and developmental strength. To emphasize mutual tolerance of the character-building aspects of indigenous group identities is, as Erikson observes, to create the sources for a strength of character crucial to a "nonviolent confrontation" that can "bring to light what insight is ready on both sides."[22] This kind of strength of character sets up an interindividual, and intergroup, dynamic that is at the heart of democratic governance.

In the absence of tolerance, democracy falls prey to demagogy and the coercion of the minority by the majority. Hitler received plebiscitary votes of approval from more than 90 percent of German voters. Yet, *with tolerance of the affirmative aspects of indigenous cultures, and a regard for basic human rights, de-*

*mocracy becomes an exercise in balancing particular sources of distinctiveness and individual difference against the universal needs of all citizens.*

Erikson's insights, and the behavioral research done subsequently, make apparent the meaning of a democratic *culture*. Recent political history provides ample illustrations of these insights. Just as a powerful parent can foreclose a child's identity achievement and lead to a reinforcement of dependence on authoritarian figures, so also can a political regime undermine social development.[23] Totalitarian governments provide one startling example, and colonial regimes another. In the aftermath of the fall of communism, just as with the collapse of fascism, populations struggle for an ethical footing from which to create a civil society that will sustain relations of mutuality and commerce.

In the same fashion, colonial and imperial regimes foreclose, through the imposition of pseudo speciation and negative identities, the widespread acquisition of strengths of character that can resist authoritarian solutions to pressing social problems.[24] Basil Davidson points out that colonialism in Africa effectively arrested the transition from traditional to modern forms of economic and political relations. Davidson shows how the racist stereotypes that bolstered apartheid were founded in observations of the reactions of traditional societies to the intervention of trade and commerce into subsistence economies. Witchcraft in Africa, for example, mimicked forms found in European society at the time of a similar economic transition. In Europe, centuries of internal struggle and warfare gave birth to the institutions of modern political economy. In Africa, the difference was that colonial regimes often used stereotypes of "primitivism" to deny the possibility of indigenous modernization, and even when intentions were benign, these regimes devalued or frustrated the indigenous social processes by which modernization might have occurred.[25]

In China, the combined impact of foreign troops, opium traders, and Christian missionaries degraded, whether intentionally or not, the structures of identity derived from China's feudal past. These interventions also set up conflicts among modernizing forces within Chinese society, most notably in the struggles between Westernizers and traditional influences and between the Chinese Nationalists and the Maoists.[26] The complex encounter between Chinese and Western values continues to shape the struggle to create a postcommunist society and regime.[27]

The loss of identity that accompanied the collapse of totalitarianism, imperialism, and colonialism is now at the core of problems in the successor nations. In contemporary Russia, rampant corruption and crime seem to accompany the effort to introduce notions of entrepreneurship and private ownership of the means of production. Communist ideology provided for little, if any, separation between the identity of a private entrepreneur and that of a thief. As a replacement for the identity ideal of the communist "comrade," nationalist forms of identity in ethnic enclaves become the source of violent political struggles.

In Africa, a similar pattern of crime, corruption, and authoritarian responses is accompanied by a search for positive forms of racially based identity. The struggle now is to escape the legacy of colonialism through indigenous means of establishing competence, integrity, and mutuality without lapsing into leader cults and repression. One recent proposal by African scholar Ali Mazrui is that African states that have demonstrated competence in political institution building, economic development, cultural achievement, and military affairs take responsibility for guiding neighboring states in these matters. By building on African-based examples and appealing to shared cultural memories and traditions, the focus will be on native means of confronting the challenges of modernity.[28]

# Conclusion:
# Identity and the State in Perspective

As is now apparent, political formations have a considerable impact on identity, but they do not constitute identity, except in extreme cases. The state can, as we see in the next chapter, limit or prevent the pathologies of discrimination, exploitation, and domination by means of coercion, example, or the indirect effect of policies that remove the conditions for the emergence of these pathologies.

Similarly, the state can play a constructive role in providing developmentally critical choices to individuals who do not have essential options available. Policies in areas of child care, education, health, and economic opportunity play a crucial role in enriching the environments within which identity is formed.

But the state cannot provide an identity to its citizens —where it has done so, it has displaced internal processes of maturation and growth by substituting identity foreclosure, as in colonialism, the replication of stereotypes, as in nationalism, and the resulting negative identities for "aliens," "foreigners," and even "natives." Identity formation takes place primarily in *civil society*, rather than through the state or even the economy. As Alan Wolfe finds in comparing social conditions in Scandinavia and the United States, wherever the state, or the market, takes over essential life functions from civil society, social conditions deteriorate.[29] In Scandinavia, he finds that both children and the elderly become the wards of an increasingly impersonal bureaucracy. In the United States, he finds a pattern of family breakdown caused by the intrusion of commercial values.[30]

What is needed is a method for avoiding the extremes. The perversion of group relatedness into aggressive pseudo speciation, as the research on authoritarian and stereotypical thinking illustrates, is seemingly at least as easy as the selective reinforcement of those aspects of group identity that are productive. We now turn to the question of how democracy may be constituted so as to become just such a method.

In the next chapter, we move to a discussion of the practical dimensions of the state's role in developing useful policies to support healthy identity development. In chapter 5, the question of multiculturalism is addressed, and in chapter 6 we explore the relationship between democracy and identity formation and address the problem of democratizing nondemocratic societies and situations.

# Notes

1. The point is similar to observations of the effect of ideology by Martin Heidegger. See Fred Dallmayr, "Postmetaphysics and Democracy," *Political Theory* 21, no. 1 (February 1993): 123. While Heidegger differs with Freud's reductionist approach to psychosomatics, Heidegger's view would seem to be more congenial to Erikson's psychosocial approach. Cf. Fred Dallmayr, "Heidegger and Freud," *Political Psychology* 14, no. 2 (June, 1993): 235–53.

2. Erik Erikson, *Childhood and Society* (New York: Norton, 1950, 1963), 185–86.

3. Angela Davis, *Women, Race, and Class* (New York: Vintage Books, 1981), 101.

4. Patricia Hill Collins, *Black Feminist Thought: Knowledge, Consciousness, and the Politics of Empowerment* (Boston: Unwin Hyman, 1990), 201–2. Cf. Erikson, *Childhood,* 404–5; Erik Erikson, *Insight and Responsibility: Lectures on the Ethical Implications of Psychoanalytic Insight* (New York: Norton, 1964), 126; idem, *Identity: Youth and Crisis* (New York: Norton, 1968), 41–42; idem, *Gandhi's Truth* (New York: Norton, 1969), 432.

5. Erikson, *Gandhi's Truth,* 390–91. Cf. Erikson, *Childhood,* 315–16; idem, *Insight and Responsibility,* 233.

6. Erik Erikson, "Conversations with Huey P. Newton," in *In Search of Common Ground,* ed. Kai Erikson (New York: Norton, 1973).

7. Erikson, *Identity,* 189; Erik Erikson, *Young Man Luther* (New York: Norton, 1958), 219; Erikson, *Gandhi's Truth,* 434.

8. Erikson, *Childhood,* 242.

9. In Robert Coles, *Erik H. Erikson: The Growth of His Work* (Boston: Atlantic, Little Brown, 1970), 181.

10. J.E. Marcia et al., *Ego Identity: A Handbook for Psychosocial Research* (New York: Springer Verlag, 1993), 8.

11. James Marcia, "The Status of the Statuses: Research Review," in Marcia et al., *Ego Identity,* 23. Marcia's citations include works by himself, Friedman, Matteson, Schenkel, Streitmatter, and Pate over a period of twenty-five years. He also notes the finding by Podd that in the Milgram obedience experiments, identity *foreclosures* were those who were most willing to administer the maximum electrical shock to what they thought were "experimental subjects" at the prompting of "psychologists."

12. Ibid.; cf. James E. Marcia, "Ego Identity Status: Relationship to Change in Self-Esteem, General Maladjustment, and Authoritarianism," *Journal of Personality* 35, no. 1 (1967): 119–33.

13. Erikson's duality of positive and negative identities makes coherent the earlier Freudian discussion of reaction formations, repression, and projection. As Anna Freud suggested, these are primarily *de-*

*fensive* mechanisms of the ego. Anna Freud, *The Ego and the Mechanisms of Defense*, trans. Cecil Baines (New York: International Universities Press, 1966), 73–74. The objects of defensive ego activities are, following Erikson, negative identifications.

14. Richard Evans, *Dialogue with Erik Erikson* (New York: Dutton, 1967), 36; Erikson, *Identity*, 203.

15. Empirical research indicates that a strong sense of self-esteem can overcome negative stereotyping of one's ethnic identity. Jean S. Phinney, Victor Chavira, and Jerry D. Tate, "The Effect of Ethnic Threat on Ethnic Self-Concept and Own-Group Ratings," *Journal of Social Psychology* 133, no. 4 (1993): 469–78. The question of redeeming ethnically distinct individuals from the pressures of culturally presented negative identities would seem to turn on the achievement of competence and integrity by other means.

16. Ibid.

17. Cf. Marcia et al., *Ego Identity*, 5.

18. Jean S. Phinney, "Ethnic Identity in Adolescents and Adults: Review of Research," *Psychological Bulletin* 1108, no. 3 (1990): 499–514.

19. For some interesting empirical evidence on this point, see Donald M. Taylor, David J. McKiman, John Christian, and Luc LaMarche, "Cultural Insecurity and Attitudes toward Multiculturalism and Ethnic Groups in Canada," *Canadian Ethnic Studies* 11, no. 2 (1979): 19–30; Wallace E. Lambert, Lambros Mermigis, and Donald M. Taylor, "Greek Canadians' Attitudes toward Own Group and Other Canadian Ethnic Groups: A Test of the Multiculturalism Hypothesis," *Canadian Journal of Behavioural Sciences* 18, no. 11 (January 1986): 35–51.

20. Nancie Caraway, *Segregated Sisterhood: Racism and the Politics of American Feminism* (Knoxville: University of Tennessee Press, 1991), 188–89.

21. Jon Michael Spencer, "Trends of Opposition to Multiculturalism," *Black Scholar* 23 (Winter/Spring 1993): 2–5; Henry Louis Gates, "A Response: Multiculturalism and Its Discontents," *Black Scholar* 24 (Winter 1994): 16–17.

22. Erikson, *Gandhi's Truth*, 439. Empirical studies of the ability of adolescents to achieve cross-cultural understanding appear to support Erikson's theory. Jean S. Phinney, Victor Chavira, and Lisa Williamson, "Acculturation Attitudes and Self-Esteem among High School and College Students," *Youth and Society* 23, no. 3 (March 1992): 299–312.

23. While the "identity crisis" is specific, in Erikson's epigenetic chart, to late adolescence, the manner in which it is dealt with has lifelong consequences for attitudes and behavior. See Marcia et al., *Ego Identity*, 58–59.

24. Marcia and Waterman cite research in the early 1970s that suggests that the higher incidence of identity foreclosure among black

high school students versus Caucasians resulted from discriminatory stereotyping by whites. See ibid., 53.

25. Basil Davidson, *The African Genius: An Introduction to African Social and Cultural History* (Boston: Little, Brown, 1969), 125–26; cf. David Martin and Phyllis Johnson, *The Struggle for Zimbabwe* (London: Faber and Faber, 1981), 51–72, on the minimal nature of educational and economic opportunity in the "best" of African colonial cases; and, on the political response, Vernon Johnson, *National Political Science Review* (1995): 5.

26. Jonathan D. Spence, *The Gate of Heavenly Peace: The Chinese and Their Revolution 1895–1980* (London: Penguin, 1981), 58–93. Cf. Fang Lizhi, *Bringing Down the Great Wall: Writings on Science, Culture and Democracy* (New York: Norton, 1990), 276–98.

27. See the analysis by Kristen Parris in chapter 8 for an application of this analysis to contemporary developments.

28. Ali Mazrui, "Cultural Amnesia, Cultural Nostalgia and False Memory: Africa's Identity Crisis Revisited" (paper presented to the symposium sponsored by the African Political Science Association and the Research Committee on Political Philosophy of the International Political Science Association in Harare, Zimbabwe, 16–18 August 1995). Mazrui points out that the historical claim that there is a distinctive "European" historical root is as dubious as the claim that there is an "African" root. In fact, both were intermixed linguistically and culturally from their beginnings as Mediterranean civilizations. Nevertheless, these political entities do have a meaning at the psychological level, a meaning that can be harnessed for constructive purposes.

29. Alan Wolfe, *Whose Keeper? Social Science and Moral Obligation* (Berkeley: University of California Press, 1989).

30. Ibid., 58–77, 162–67.

# 4

# Identity and Human Development

Just as with the term *identity,* the word *politics* has its familiar associations: legislatures, leaders, lobbyists, voters, and all the complex ways that they interact. We have developed sophisticated institutions for working through the competing pressures and myriad interests of individuals and groups. Political analysis conventionally focuses on individual choices and how these choices are brought together through political processes to shape decisions. What animates this institutional structure is ideas, or images that people have of what they want or think they need or deserve.

Conventional political analysis focuses on the individual material desires people have, yet history is filled with examples of material sacrifice in the name of psychological motivations: solidarity, nationalism, vengeance, not to mention honor. The ideas put forward as justifications for sacrifice always have a social character; they appeal to shared moral principles, loyalties, and social bonds of various kinds.

What is missing in conventional analysis is a way of linking individual motivation with the intrinsically social nature of human life so that we can account for the whole range of political behavior while, at the same time, suggesting directions for public policy that will make life better for everyone. We know that individual choices are not made in isolation; individual choices are cued, shaped, and constrained by powerful influences emanating from social forces great and small. Yet it is also clear that choices are never entirely the product of the social environment. There is at least an element of autonomy.

45

To understand these transactions, we need to see the *patterns* evident in the choices people make. What are the consistent elements in motivation? Why? How can these motivations be dealt with in political terms that will yield benign results and avoid exploitation and violence? The answers to these questions may be found in what we call *identity analysis.*

## Individualists versus Developmentalists

There is a shift in political thinking underway. As Nancy Rosenblum and Sheryl Turkle note, "the heart of the change can be simply stated: unlike standard notions of person as chooser or moral agent, the self has emerged as reflective, developmental, and relational."[1] We do make choices, but they are not made in isolation or on a moral plane separated from the rest of our mental universe.

Choices are manifestations of a developmental impetus arising from internal drives and reflections, on one side, and the possibilities that society presents, on the other. While no analysis cannot account for every variation, we can see the underlying pattern of issues on the individual side. Adult criminal behavior, for example, is highly correlated with the experience of an abusive childhood. On the social side, we can identify patterns of response that lead, in often predictable directions, toward certain kinds of results. As an illustration, constitutional democracies have a better track record than dictatorships in protecting individual rights.

What is meant here by *identity analysis* is that the search for competence, integrity, and mutuality, which reaches a critical stage in late adolescence and early adulthood, in fact becomes the key to the lifelong patterns of motivation we all share. By working out the ways that politically determined policies can have an impact on the developmental environment, we can begin to see how to respond to these motivations in a developmentally constructive fashion.

*Here is the sense in which identity analysis leads to politics in a new key.* Identity is a thread that binds self and society. As material creatures, we could live quite well in an amply provisioned isolation. As humans, we need the interaction society affords to manifest our essential being. Material provision is, of course, a critical aspect of society, but it is not the only, or even the most powerful, reason for the existence of social institutions. The question is, what does this mean for political processes and public policy?

Perhaps the central struggle of twentieth-century Western political thought has been to develop a conception of the human condition that can support a redefinition of politics so that democracy becomes its central characteristic. As suggested in chapter 1, one's approach to understanding democracy turns on whether one takes a developmentalist or an individualist point of view. The argument in this book is that the human condition is characterized by a developmental sequence involving known needs, aspirations, and behaviors. Individualists, in contrast, take the position that the uncertainty and open-endedness of human nature defy systematic understanding.

For the individualists, democracy is about dealing with inevitable conflicts and differences. For the developmentalists, democracy is a strategy for locating the shared characteristics of human nature. Democratic means are ways of finding agreement on underlying commonalities.

What does the psychoanalytic tradition have to contribute to this discussion? Sigmund Freud saw motivation in terms of psychosexual drives. These "drives" or instincts were different only in the nature of the objects of desire from the material acquisitiveness of the property-seeking individualist of classical liberalism. Erikson changes the metaphor behind psychiatry to an image of *transactive psychosocial development*. This has profound political consequences. In doing so, he draws psychiatric theory away from its uses alternately as a rationale for repressive institutions and as a manifesto for individual instinctual liberation. And he sets the stage for a form of political analysis that is markedly different from the individualist version of "who gets what, when, and how," to use Harold Lasswell's memorable definition of politics.

There is, according to Erik Erikson, such a thing as psychosocial equilibrium and, with it, the promise that "the freshness and wholeness of experience arising with a resolved crisis can, in an ongoing life, transcend trauma and defense."[2] Rather than simply response to instinct or unloading of internal pressures on the environment, human life is conceived of in developmental terms. The dividend of developmental strength, as we have seen in the previous chapter, is a *sense of humanity* that can sponsor forms of social progress.[3] Therein lies the possibility that understanding identity will lead to broader political insight as well as better politics.

## Identity Analysis and Identity Politics

By understanding identity as a concept distinct from its "identity politics," operationalizations as class, gender, and race, we can begin to see how the interplay of all these elements depends on fundamental issues of competence, integrity, and mutuality. Each of these elements provides guideposts to political processes and public policies.

Before we can understand the full power of *identity analysis*, it is necessary to retrieve the political meaning of identity from some of its misleading uses in *identity politics*. As we see, the current focus on class, gender, and race as synonyms for identity obscures the progressive possibilities evident in the formulation of identity presented here.

To see identity as the equivalent of class is to engage in economic and sociological determinism of a kind that leaves only class conflict as a solution to political problems. While this may be warranted in given historical situations, recent history has shown us that regimes that rule in the name of class are just as likely to be repressive as those that rule in the name of race. Similarly, identity-as-gender in a militant essentialist form leads away from the institutions and practices that make it possible for both sexes to live together on the basis of shared needs and interests.

It is not the radicalism of the race, gender, class version of identity politics that is problematic, it is the one-sidedness of the concept of identity that underlies this formulation. What is

48

missing is a way of seeing the dynamism and the possibilities for progressive change involved in the tension between the negative and positive identity elements, the particular and the universal, the given and the possible. What is needed is an account that reveals the necessity for cooperation as well as conflict.

We see how each of these versions of identity appears in a broader, more useful framework as we focus, in the remainder of this chapter, on how to enable the development of competence, integrity, and mutuality. Each aspect of identity carries with it the need for supportive political policies and processes. In chapter 5, we see how identity analysis provides the key to understanding the politics of multiculturalism. Finally, in chapter 6, we return to the question of democracy—how can a democratic society discover and act on developmental insights so as to minimize the use of coercive power and maximize developmental freedom?

## *Competence:*
## Identity and the Market

Adam Smith's essential defense of the market is that it rewards competence—competence in meeting the demands of consumers. The efficient worker who can produce a commodity for a lower price is rewarded. The worker who labors to satisfy demand for a product also, according to identity analysis, fulfills a developmental requirement by demonstrating competence, and in a way that sustains mutuality by taking care of the needs of others. Thus the market, by rewarding labor, is potentially the friend of human development.

The question identity-as-class raises is about how the distribution of economic rewards fits with the achievement of competence, the enhancement of integrity, and the sustenance of mutuality. Economic "means" are just that—means to these developmental ends. To resolve, through class warfare, differences in the distribution of these economic means leads into the repressive political environment that classical liberals, as well as conservatives, would criticize.

Just as the forceful leveling of socioeconomic distinctions

leads to repressive politics, so also does an unregulated market distort the support structure for encouraging positive identity development. It is as artificial to reward individuals for being lucky, or privileged by birth, as it is to equalize their material wealth in the name of doctrinal commitment to equality.

The market rewards capital, whether acquired by labor, fraud, chance, inheritance, or the proceeds of a monopolistic or oligopolistic position in the marketplace. All but the first of these has no standing in developmental theory, with the exception of those limited forms of inheritance that contribute to the maintenance of the family. The forces of capital reinforced by political power can violate developmental norms just as surely as egalitarian regimes intent on erasing authentic differences among people.

The problem is not with the market as a device but with the substitution of market devices for other social and political processes that are essential to human development. The practices and customs of civil society that give relations of mutuality a higher priority than individual material advancement, for example, are characteristic of a civilized society.[4] That is why the family enjoys a protected status that constrains individual choices about the use of one's material resources.

What identity analysis has to offer, then, is a theory of market regulation and constraint. Viewed from a developmental perspective, those aspects of the market that encourage the cultivation and maintenance of competence are socially beneficial. Those forms of buying and selling that undermine the social structures that support competence are harmful. We know that limits must be placed on child labor, for example, because it can undermine education and health, both of which are critical to achieving competence in a broad array of human activities. As we see below, there are other measures for the regulation of the market arising from considerations of integrity and mutuality.

## Integrity:
## Developing Shared Meanings

The essence of human development lies in the shared meanings that individuals create or acquire. Paradoxically, individuation is meaningless without the social recognition of distinctiveness. That is why so much of behavior is a form of "acting." Just as actors seek an audience by creating a role, so do all of us have an "act" that contains our characteristic mannerisms, traits, styles, and modes of behavior. Absent an audience, our "act" has no meaning.

As any actor knows, the challenge is to reach across the edge of the stage to bring the audience into the play. In an effective performance, shared meanings become so pervasive that the audience, the actors, and the playwright find, at the end, that they are integrated into a world that makes a new kind of sense. Applause and bows are the result.

These moments of solidarity, whether in the theater, on the sports field, in a political demonstration, or in an everyday exchange of pleasantries, illustrate the search for integrity (or, again, integral-ity) that occupies such a large place on the developmental agenda. What we badly want to do is to paint a picture of the world that shows where each of us fits—a picture that is recognized and shared by others.

The political manifestations of this urge are everywhere to be seen. *Nations* of people organize around ties of ethnicity expressed politically, artistically, literarily, and even gastronomically. *States*, generally composed of nations, make citizens of their subjects and integrate them into frameworks of roles, rights, and responsibilities embodied in law. *Ideologies* gather up philosophical positions, symbols of power, visions of the future, and programs of action in a grand synthesis that places each of us in a comprehensible world.

So important is this activity that religions and cultures set aside one day of the week, not just to rest, but to put the world together through worship of some ideal conception of it. But how can we capture the specific aspects of this phenomenon through identity analysis? Clearly not all forms of solidarity are good for development, nor are all forms of antisocial individualism bad.

The benchmarks of developmentally sustaining ideologies are those that affirm essential developmental traits in all people. Fascism, as an example of a destructive ideology, was built on racist denigration, nationalist chauvinism, and authoritarianism. Competence was ascribed to genetic superiority, integrity to service to the nation's goals, and mutuality was subordinated to obedience. The hollowness of the identities shaped by fascist allegiance, and the pathologies that accompanied them, are amply documented.[5]

To add a more systematic level of understanding requires that we see the need for integrality underlying all forms of ideology. To argue the case at the extremes, consider regimes where religion is either proscribed, as in Leninist Russia, or made coercive through the power of the state, as in contemporary Iran. In the former case, people are deprived of the sustenance that institutions can bring to faith—which is perhaps the most fundamental of our attachments to the world around us. In the latter, the continuity and sustenance that religion provides is enforced rather than accepted through faith.

## *Mutuality:*
## Politics in the Affirmative

Governments may not be able to make people love one another—indeed, they have often been rather better at helping people hate one another. But the political context for human development has a lot to do with all manner of relations of mutuality. Marriage and divorce are civil institutions sanctioned by law. Public policy has a lot to do with making families viable, for example: AFDC, minimum-wage laws, unemployment compensation, survivors insurance, and Social Security. But how can we establish the meaning and boundaries of mutuality as a political concept? Isn't it just an invitation to unlimited government meddling in essentially private matters?

The answer to this question has to take account of our cultural heritage. In this individualistic political culture, the role of government has been conceived, alternately, as simply removing obstacles to personal freedom or, in its more progressive mode, as positively enabling individuals to have the means of making choices. These conceptions of negative and positive liberty have been argued over for more than a century. Classical liberalism was built on the notion that, through constitutional restraints and the specification of a system of individual rights, individuals could pursue their own development free of government interference—and of threats of violence from their neighbors. Negative liberty lies at the core of classical liberalism and contemporary conservative libertarianism, and it receives expression as a celebration of the "free" market and the minimization of government power.

Positive liberty, by contrast, is the essential concept for progressive liberals and democratic socialists. This concept sponsors the regulatory role of government and the welfare state. The argument is that the government must be an active force in mediating and constraining exercises of private power. The policy limitations encountered under the negative liberty rubric have been overridden by the complexities of modern industrial cultures. Yet it is also true that the lack of boundaries for institutional power arising from a positive liberty perspective create dangers of repression, bureaucratization, and inefficiency in the allocation of resources. How can the concept of mutuality help resolve this conundrum?

The political struggle of this past century in the democratic West has centered on whether, in the name of negative liberty, governments have refused to face up to economic crises, the ills of poverty, the destruction of the environment, and the exploitation of human life in the labor market and elsewhere. Alternately, in periods of leftist dominance, the issues center on whether positive government has become too intrusive, wasteful, inefficient, and counterproductive.[6]

The problem with this debate is its either/or character. One side clings to the autonomous morally independent individual.[7] The other argues that the individual is the creature of social forces. The first ignores or diminishes the role of society and therefore denigrates the importance of government. The second treats people as puppets and deprives them of character and motivation, while placing faith in democratic governance as a way of regulating social power. The cyclical and repetitive nature of these disputes suggests that there is a flaw in the conceptual foundations of the arguments.

Mutuality, seen as an element of identity, brings to this discussion a new conceptual possibility. We have defined the concept in terms of "the attachments that make possible a sense of personal continuity" (see chap. 2). What are the politically relevant forms of these attachments? Surely the state should not be responsible for love relationships!

The answer to this question requires a bit of perspective on how we currently link basic human drives to social forms and institutions. Each of our drives has its institutional expression. Sex, love, and procreation are bound up in the institutions of marriage and the family and in laws that regulate sexual behavior. Work becomes politically relevant as a job, occupation, or profession and, indirectly, as property. Faith finds its institutional expression in religion and churches.

By legally constituting the institutions and social forms arising from these drives, government acquires the ability to regulate them for social purposes. Religions are protected in the First Amendment to the Constitution, property in the Fifth and Fourteenth amendments among other places, and the family and marriage are the cornerstones of laws governing private relations. So the question in this, or any other modern democracy, is not *whether* government should regulate individual life, but *how much* and *for what purposes?*

At this point the hollowness of the conventional analysis becomes apparent. If government is only about ensuring the sanctity of private property, then how do we explain the complex web that governments weave around the most intimate of daily activities having to do with our physical and mental health, familial relations, education, and the protection and limitation of religious practices? Is the family nothing more than a property relationship, or does it have a moral claim different from other forms of association? Why should an employer be held responsible for anything more than a worker's wages? Yet our attempts at regulation address in only the most haphazard way these qualitative and, as is argued here, developmentally significant dimensions of the issues.

What about the economy? The essential aspect of the economy from a developmental point of view is the way that it organizes work. Material provision is the focus of much talk about the economy, but it is clear that systems for supplying goods and services to meet demands can take many forms, from command economies through to self-sufficient communities of hunter-gatherers. While the economists' version of efficiency (getting the most output from the least input of resources) differentiates these systems, so also does their propensity to engage and shape developmental processes. While the economists' version of efficiency may permit us to rate the performance of an economic system at any given moment, the real question has to do with the performance of economic institutions over a longer period of time. A "command economy" or an unfettered "market economy" may be very efficient, in this sense, for a short period of time or under the special circumstances of a war, but what institutions of political economy will last over time?

We know that a command economy will generate inefficiencies and corruption in time, and a completely free economy will legitimize fraud and theft if left unregulated. Both maladies arise from an imperfect fit between the logic of human development and the logic of efficient resource provision. A command economy fails because it frustrates and inhibits individual initiative and engagement. The latter is Adam Smith's essential point. Similarly, a market economy runs into trouble because it cannot adjust to values that arise from protecting processes of human development or processes of environmental preservation. The turn toward a regulated economy at the beginning of this century was powered by a reaction to monopolistic combinations, the abuse of child labor, and the tainting of the food supply. All of these involve problems of human motivation and social responsibility.

What does identity analysis offer for understanding the economy? For political purposes, a job is to work as the institution of the family is to sex and love. The job makes of work a political and social institution. In the economists' calculus, there is only work, that is, the provision of labor as an input to the productive process. In this view, the worker has no status that differentiates her or him from the raw materials or machinery that are also part of the productive process. An employee who has a job, in contrast, is involved in a social-political relationship with other people—a relationship constructed implicitly on the presumption that the job ought somehow to provide for survival. For this reason, family "benefits" are often attached to jobs, and we speak of "living wages." The minimum-wage legislation that has such a powerful influence on the question of poverty is a leading illustration of the political significance of this view.

If a central drive has to do with the achievement and validation of competence, and with making a "place" in the world that sustains one's sense of integration as well as feeds one's family, then the *job* becomes a key institution. Jobs are ways, among other things, of sharing risks arising from fluctuations in the need for work between the employee and the person who profits from labor, the capitalist.[8] We know from research on factory closings that unemployment compensation can tide over a person's family, but it is very difficult to break through the psychological shell constructed by someone whose purpose in living has been undercut.

What emerges from this analysis is a rationale for minimum-wage legislation, the protection of employees from arbitrary dismissal, prior notification of factory closings, and a range of other job-related protections. While the employer does not "owe" the employee a job, it can be argued on this view that there is a social interest in defining the minimal circumstances under which one human being can profit from the labor of another. That minimum has to do with not undermining essential aspects of the developmental process. Similarly, slavery and prostitution are versions of labor marketing that vitiate the ties of integrity and mutuality that undergird human development. Herein lies the role of the state that, through democratic processes of legislation and adjudication, can provide the community with the means of defining those minimums.

As for the corporation, which operates as a voluntary actor beyond these minimums, there is much more to be learned from identity analysis about what really motivates and engages the best efforts of employees over the longer term. Small wonder that newer, more intelligent corporations are less hierarchical, more likely to offer profit sharing, cognizant of the need for childcare and parental leave, and nurturing of a participative corporate culture where teamwork replaces command relationships. What this trend suggests is that the trade-off between protection of minimum standards and market demands for productivity is not a zero-sum game, as some conservative rhetoricians suggest. In the longer term, a degraded and debilitated workforce earning starvation wages with no job protection will be less productive than an engaged, motivated, and involved team of employees who have a stake in the future of the corporation. By using minimum standards to protect progressive corporations from being undercut in the short term by unscrupulous competitors, the partnership between government and business can yield a better developmental climate in which competitiveness is enhanced.

The essential aspect of this analysis is that the market provides a social test for the value of what is produced, while a democratic political system provides a social test for assessing the human consequences of job environments. These two processes need to work in balance if we are to avoid all the social costs of a debased workforce, on the one hand, or, on the other, an economy that degenerates into stagnation because of excessive government regulation and corruption.

Something of the same frame of analysis can be applied to the question of community responsibilities for the family. Families have been created in law largely as property relations, with some additional protections from physical and emotional abuse. In the absence of satisfactory ways of using the metaphor of property to deal with parent-child relations, for example, our legal system simply vests the power to decide specific equities in special courts and judges. What is missing is a coherent rationale for community intervention into situations where families are absent, failing, or dysfunctional to their members.

Once again, the essential point about identity analysis is that the community and its agent, the state, cannot provide the substance of relations of mutuality. Bonds of kinship and personal commitment exist in a realm separate from the conscious and deliberate organization of the community to secure the well-being of its members. What the community *can* do is three things: (1) avoid undercutting the family; (2) reinforce the family by making constructive choices available where they otherwise would not be present; and (3) control the abuses of family relations, some of which include treating people as property.

The sustenance of committed relations between partners, children, and siblings serves the purposes of human development by avoiding the alienation, isolation, and self-doubt occasioned by the failure of these relations. This sort of sustenance requires both a well-constructed and accountable system for dealing with the abuse of these relations and the provision of support for their development. Where these relations have failed and left children, in particular, in developmentally vulnerable situations, remedial action is called for through a combination of public and private means.

The indifference to mutuality that results from radical individualism leads to the kind of social breakdown and anomie found among the impoverished, the transient, and the abandoned. These conditions are found most frequently in ghettoes and rural areas, but are by no means confined to them. The implication of this analysis for the planning of communities is that they need to be established with the social stability of the population firmly in mind. A generation of experience with huge low-income housing developments such as East Saint Louis's Pruitt-Igoe and Chicago's Cabrini Green, as well as with anonymous suburbs of single-class dwellings, suggests that social mechanisms for encouraging upward mobility and community intermediation are vital to healthy possibilities for community development.

## Conclusion:
## The Uses of Identity Analysis

Having marked out the parameters of identity as competence, integrity, and mutuality, it is time to return to our earlier theme about the contest between the developmentalists and the individualists over the parameters of democratic governance (see chap. 1). Viewed from the perspective of political theory, the concept of a developmental pattern in human life could open up the possibility of enforced conformity, the marginalization of "different" people, and the collapse, ultimately, of democracy itself. The use of psychiatric norms for these purposes can be easily illustrated.

Nevertheless, the latent assumption of the individualist approach is that, in the absence of governance, freedom will prevail. With all that we know from inquiries about human interdependence, whether behavioral or philosophical, interpretive or scientific, the fact is that we are inalienably social creatures. The only question is, in what field of social forces will our choices will be shaped?

The resolution of this debate is through identity analysis. In each application, identity as a phenomenon appears to involve a tension between particular and universal elements, and a recognition that identity resides in the space *between* individual drives and social responses. To focus only on one end of these transactions is to miss the political dynamics of identity formation. How, then, can the processes of democracy become instruments of an affirmation of human development? That is the topic of the final two chapters in this part.

## Notes

1. Nancy Rosenblum and Sherry Turkle, "Political Philosophy's Psychologized Self: Speaking Prose without Knowing It," in *Critical Issues in Social Thought*, ed. Murray Milgate (New York: Academic Press, 1989), 48.

2. Erik H. Erikson, *Insight and Responsibility: Lectures on the Ethical Implications of Psychoanalytic Insight* (New York: Norton, 1964), 276.

3. Erik H. Erikson, *Childhood and Society* (New York: Norton, 1950, 1963), 412.

4. Adam Smith would clearly agree with this. In his famous formulation of the "sympathy principle" in *The Theory of Moral Sentiments* he describes how social bonds are made from the desire to secure the sympathy of others through engaging in actions that evoke associations of suffering or, alternatively, of heroism and self-sacrifice. This amounts to a preliminary description of what is meant, in identity analysis, by mutuality. Smith clearly regards these ties as more socially useful than mere economic advantage.

5. Theodore Adorno, *The Authoritarian Personality* (New York: Harper, 1950).

6. Albert Hirschman details the repetitive, almost cyclic, pattern of conservative claims about the futility of progressive reforms, the perverse effects of the reforms, and the jeopardy they create for those they are trying to help. He also notes the similar character of defenses made

of progressivism. See Albert Hirschman, *The Rhetoric of Reaction* (Cambridge: Harvard University Press, 1991).

7. See Chiaki Nishiyama and Kurt Leube, *The Essence of Hayek* (Palo Alto, Calif.: Hoover Institution Press, 1984), 63.

8. This point was made by Tom Walker in an e-mail exchange.

# 5

# Identity, Multiculturalism, and Conflict Resolution

We have, until now, taken it for granted that the rhythms of development are common to all people. Yet the persistence of differences based on race, nationality, gender, class, and religion has been the most striking feature of post–Cold War politics. The common characteristic of conflicts in Eastern Europe, Africa, the Middle East—or in American cities—is that, for many people, group-based differences undermine the ties of universal community. If, as I suggested earlier, there is a universal framework for human development, then there is a basis for resolving these conflicts through action based on an understanding of identity needs.

In the ferocity of internecine conflict, there is clearly something at issue besides economic advantage. The destruction that these conflicts have wrought can hardly be seen as economically advantageous to anyone. If, indeed, political conflict was primarily the result of economic differences, as endemic and profound as they are, the world would be a far more violent place than it is. What identity analysis demonstrates is that, independently of economic advantage or disadvantage, considerations of identity have the potential *both* to tear communities apart and bring them together.

What has been dropped out of much current discussion are all the possibilities in the conceptualization of identity that point to the peaceful resolution of conflict, or at least the uncovering of shared interests. Conflict, and contested identities, occupy a preferential position in contemporary political theorizing. While conflict may be essential to the escape from oppression as a political phenomenon, the scholarship of identity needs to have in place a model that embraces the full potential of the concept. Cooperation is every bit as essential to identity formation as conflict.

When identity is understood in this way, the spectrum of strategies for identity formation from separatism to universalism becomes evident, and with it comes a spectrum of political action that spans conflict and cooperation. Consequently, the task of this chapter is to illuminate the range of possibilities implicit in the phenomenon of identity and its relationships with political community. We look for the insights that point the way to the peaceful resolution of conflict and the sustenance of productive forms of development.

## Identity, Multiculturalism, and Democracy

Individual identities differ in *content*, but the evidence we have cited strongly suggests that the psychological imperative of identity formation is universal. If it can be inferred that quest for identity achievement is central to all people, then there is a powerful argument for at least a minimal form of equality as a political value. Without a common minimum of security and opportunity, and without basic social tolerance of diverse identities, individual humanness and humanity collectively are endangered.[1] Both victor and vanquished are psychologically damaged in a society that reinforces exploitation.

While minimal levels of tolerance and security are vitally important, the distinctions that cultures establish in recognizing competence, generating integrity, and supporting mutuality are also critical to the developmental process. Culture largely determines the materials available for identity formation. As Erikson notes,

> only a gradually accruing sense of identity, based on the experience of social health and cultural solidarity at the end of each major childhood crisis, promises that periodical balance in hu-

man life which—in integration of the ego states—makes for a sense of humanity. But wherever this sense is lost, wherever integrity yields to despair and disgust, wherever generativity yields to stagnation, intimacy to isolation, and identity to confusion, an array of associated infantile fears are apt to become mobilized: for only an identity safely anchored in the "patrimony" of a cultural identity can produce a workable psychosocial equilibrium.[2]

So people need culture, Erikson observes, but not too much:

The concept of ego identity may be misunderstood.... One may suspect that all identity is conformist, that a sense of identity is achieved primarily through the individual's complete surrender to given social roles and through his unconditional adaptation to the demands of social change. No ego, it is true, can develop outside of social processes which offer workable prototypes and roles. The healthy and strong individual, however, adapts these roles to the further processes of his ego, thus doing his share in keeping the social process alive.[3]

This tension between the universal and the particular in identity formation holds the analytic key to understanding the relationships between identity and politics. In this chapter, we consider how race, as an example, plays on identity needs and community politics. Having opened the issue of deep-seated differences, we explore the political implications of differentiation. Then we turn to the matter of morality. Is there any moral value implicit either in the particularities of identity or in the universalist conception that Erikson sponsored? Finally, the bottom line for political community is assessed: How can conflicts be resolved? What has identity analysis got to do with pointing the way to better communities?

# The Indigenous
# and the Universal

Race as a contributor to identity poses the issues of universality and particularity in the clearest possible form. On the side of the particularity of race, there are such facts as intrinsic differentiation, whether seen as genetic or merely as a matter of skin color. There is the massive historical experience of racism. There are the behavioral preferences that distinguish races from each other. There are commonalities of religion, politics, and culture clearly associated with race.

On the side of universality, however, are some equally impressive facts. Genetic differentiation is a minor factor in overall somatic makeup, and it is a complex and certainly diluted form of differentiation in practice. The biological framework of physical development does not seem to differ. Individual variations of ability and achievement defy racial stereotypes. Furthermore, historic experiences of racism are highly variable on closer analysis. Intraracial discrimination, the artificiality of such constructs as "African," and the variations of cultural context that influence racism all combine to weaken any determinist theory of the significance of race for identity.[4]

Yet race, like gender, remains an inescapable component of identity. This is true even if the attributes of race are made up of myth, legend, or stereotypes. As Anthony Appiah points out, "invented histories, invented biologies, invented cultural affinities come with every identity."[5] Surely nationalities are nonetheless real for being invented. At the same time it is true of race, as with gender, that the areas of overlap and shared characteristics are such that distinctions must always be seen empirically as a matter of degree and probability, rather than as rigid divisions.

What are we left with as analysts of identity? What the phenomenon of race makes evident is the fact that there can be no standardized human experience at the level of culture. Race opens our eyes, if they are clouded by a naive humanism, to the phenomenon of variation among human beings—and it does not stop with race or with gender. In fact, variation does not stop with any subset of the species. In some genetically precise sense, *each of us is a minority of one.* And all of us, when our beliefs about our identities are tested against absolute truthfulness, are at least partly fictional creatures. Variation and invention are endemic to the human constitution, but there is a constitution.

What is also endemic is a framework within which development occurs. All of us share genetic patterns, cultural similarities, social interactions, and developmental needs and aspirations. The patterns of human development do cross racial, cultural, religious, territorial, and, to some degree, gender-based lines. But the content that fills in those patterns reflects variations introduced by cultural circumstances, economic necessities, accident, and the idiosyncrasies of individual life. What we are left with is the generalized problem of *difference.*

What about individual differences? There is no more perplexing moral question than the resolution of differences between oneself and others. Political theorist William Connolly sees the problem of affirming difference as the critical political aspect of the process of identity formation.[6] In his view, identity necessarily involves difference. It is the differences that constitute the boundaries of one's identity. Though his view is based on a stipulated concept of identity, there is an intuitive appeal in this definition. For difference implies discrimination, and therein lies the link to the uses—and misuses—of power. A completion of the analysis, however, requires that we account for the fact that identities are as likely to be complementary as they are discriminatory. The capacity of humans to function in webs of myriad interdependent identifications is at least as remarkable as our penchant for the subjugation of distinctive personalities.

This, of course, is where politics comes in. What forms of human mutuality can be encouraged, even protected by law, that will minimize subjugation while fostering interdependence, or at least tolerance? Connolly rejects liberal "neutralism" as a means of meeting these challenges and offers instead an impressive repertoire of reasons for resisting conventions, structures, and forms of regulation that constrain and confine differences.[7] Still, as he implicitly acknowledges, a commitment to diversity is only the beginning of what it will take to bring about a more equitable distribution of the necessities of life.[8]

*A conceptualization of identity rooted in observation allows us to see that differences foster identity as well as threaten it.* The bridges that Erikson and Gilligan make apparent are in the transactional character of identity formation and defense. The validation of competence, the shared consciousness that constitutes the integration of meaning, and the mutuality of feeling that allows individuals to relate closely to one another are all devices that make identity and mitigate conflicts over differences at the same time. In contrast, when pseudospeciation intervenes, or negative identities are reified through the polity, identity becomes hostile to difference, and difference begins to destroy the viability of identity. These concepts allow an account of the full spectrum of the relation between identity and difference.

What identity analysis adds is support for Connolly's rejection of liberal neutralism on other grounds. Culture never can be neutral. It is an active component of every identity. No one acquires an identity in a vacuum or in the abstract. But what politics as an aspect of culture can contribute is not just tolerance but an active approach to policies that will make possible for everyone the achievement of competencies, the sustenance of mutuality, and a respect for humane ways of integrating oneself into the world. (That is the focus of the next chapter.) One issue remains, however: the question of morality. Is there anything moral about identity? Can an empirically based model of human development answer our need for moral imperatives?

# Morality and Identity

Charles Taylor, a leading North American philosopher, sees identity as the key to moral self-definition.[9] Absent a chosen sense of how we stand on key moral issues, and "some reference to a defining community," we have no identity and therefore no "self."[10] His examination of the philosophical precursors of our current self-understandings illuminates the cultural webs within which we seek moral orientation.

On the face of it, Taylor's enterprise may be distinguished from Erikson's as the difference between a venture in moral philosophy and a project emanating from natural science and behavioral observation.[11] But what Taylor has arrived at by philosophical analysis, as well as by personal involvement in the politics of Quebec and its relationships with Canada, is similar in crucial respects to what Erikson formulated on the basis of clinical research. Taylor says we must make sense of our lives because to do otherwise is to validate a life that is "incomprehensible and pathological."[12] Erikson says we seek identity because we must—we are driven by the ineluctable transaction between instinctual drives and social realities to formulate an identity as an act of the psyche. There is the hint of complementarity in Taylor's use of the term "pathological," which itself implies that there is an empirically demonstrable natural developmental pattern in human life.

What is suggested by this link can be defended on other grounds as well. Presuming the correctness of Erikson's analysis, and accepting that it illustrates as well our capacity for self-reflection, Taylor's moral orientation becomes the fulfillment, rather than the alternative, to Erikson's (and Gilligan's) project. Accurate self-reflection should indeed reveal where human nature takes us. In the grand tradition of political philosophy, Erikson reveals the natural state of the human condition, while Taylor explores the moral resolution of that condition. The "sense of humanity" that a fulfillment of the drive to identity allows promises the kind of humane moral reflection Taylor prizes.

## Ideology, Identity Analysis, and Multiculturalism

It is now time to bring this discussion of differences and morality to bear on the ideological configurations of contemporary politics. The rise of new forms of conservative politics has been the distinguishing feature of contemporary politics. Todd Gitlin notes the greater success of the right in developing a political program based on "commonalities" among people, as opposed to the fragmentation of the left consequent on the rise of identity politics. For the left, he suggests, differentiation is seen as an end in itself.[13] To the extent that the left was historically, as John Patrick Diggins argues, the party of belief in fundamental change, the new posture of the left amounts to a concession of the possibilities of change to the right.[14] That is because, without some unifying vision, the left cannot overcome the divisions and differences that alienate and immobilize the forces of protest.

On the one hand, the contemporary left evinces the humanist desire to see to the liberation of all people by removing all forms of stigmatization and embracing each diverse element of society on its own terms. On the other hand, however, is the inchoate dream of some essential humanity that will lead to peaceful coexistence and a mutual regard for the economic security of all members of the community. The latter remains a dream as long as the left has no way of working out the connections between identity and community.

Conservatives have also been beset by divisions. The right is distinguished by a curious approach to community; the underlying assumption of conservatism, of whatever kind, is that distinctions and gradations among people are the key to the well-ordered polity. As conservatives have gained power in the West, their political parties and movements have been beset by internal divisions between two concepts of how to act on this belief: one depends on traditional "family" values and the moral customs and authority structures of Western civilization, which, taken together, form a potent identity construct. The other relies on the market to serve as a vehicle of individual liberation and distinction and carries with it the identity myths of individual self-sufficiency.[15] Each conservative persuasion, the traditionalist and the individualist, has its common appeal even as it facilitates the division of people into categories of saints and sinners, independent and dependent.

Ultimately the two visions are in conflict. *Traditional* conservatism envisions an "organic" community characterized by numerous distinctions of a moral, customary, and authoritative variety. *Individualist* conservatism relies on a market that continually divides and redivides the community on the basis of a single indicator of worth: wealth. The market is no respecter of morality. And moral distinctions have no place in price theory. Individualism and social traditionalism do not easily cohabit. What begins politically as the promise of a common vision becomes a recipe for a failure of governance as divisions are exacerbated, and conflict becomes chronic. Internal divisions among conservatives had as much or more to do with the removal of Margaret Thatcher and the troubled legacy of Reaganism than the efficacy of liberals in mounting a response to them. Issues that pit choice against tradition become the fault lines of modern conservative politics: abortion, school prayer, censorship of pornography, the environment, and approaches to internationalism. All these issues divide the right internally, as well as differentiating right from left.

For conservatives of either kind, the commitment to "commonalities" is thus a bit of an illusion. It is quite possible to be rich at the expense of another, or to deem oneself morally superior by condemning another. The traditionalist image is one that implicitly favors one culture, and very nearly one race, over others. The individualist image avoids the problems of race, gender, and class by resolving all issues into a matter of individual striving. Taken by itself, neither deals with the world as we know it: a global community in which race, gender, religion, nationality, class, and culture are very real indeed, and in which the moral superiority of one over another cannot be easily demonstrated.

But identity is not a zero-sum game. Identity achieved by victimization is pathology. As we have shown, identity formation, and human development generally, is an essentially transactive process composed simultaneously of individual striving and social support. A politics based on human development, rather than on material gain or moral absolutes, has the possibility of fostering commonalities that endure.

If this view of identity formation as the cornerstone of a new conception of multiculturalism is taken as significant, then what is needed is a method for implementing this vision. In the next chapter, we turn to the question of how democracy can function to make real the possibilities of a constructive conception of human development. We also explore the policy implications of identity analysis.

## Notes

1. Erik H. Erikson, *Gandhi's Truth* (New York: Norton, 1969), 244.
2. Erik H. Erikson, *Childhood and Society* (New York: Norton, 1950, 1963), 412.

3. Ibid.

4. Kwame Anthony Appiah, *In My Father's House: Africa in the Philosophy of Culture* (New York: Oxford University Press, 1992).

5. Ibid., 174.

6. William Connolly, *Identity/Difference: Democratic Negotiations of Political Paradox* (Ithaca, N.Y.: Cornell University Press, 1991).

7. Ibid., chap. 6.

8. Ibid., 214.

9. Charles Taylor, *Sources of the Self: The Making of the Modern Identity* (Cambridge: Harvard University Press, 1989), 27, 33.

10. Ibid., 34–36.

11. The question of the is/ought gulf is clearly at issue here. For present purposes, I would simply point out that behavioral generalizations of the following sort are used as justification for otherwise philosophical analyses by Connolly and Taylor: "The relation of individuality to foreknowledge of death creates an ambiguous context for the exercise of freedom." Connolly, *Identity/Difference*, 17. "The very way we walk, move, gesture, speak is shaped from the earliest moments by our awareness that we appear before others, that we stand in public space, and this space is potentially one of respect or contempt, shame or pride." Taylor, *Sources of the Self*, 15. If this sort of evidence is to be introduced, then why not be systematic in taking account of empirical research of the kind developmental psychology offers? Cf. Kenneth Hoover and Todd Donovan, *The Elements of Social Scientific Thinking*, 6th ed. (New York: St. Martin's, 1995), chap. 6.

12. Taylor, *Sources of the Self*, 32.

13. Todd Gitlin, "The Left, Lost in the Politics of Identity," *Harper's Magazine*, September 1993, 16–20.

14. John Diggins, *The Rise and Fall of the American Left* (New York: Norton, 1992).

15. Kenneth Hoover and Raymond Plant, *Conservative Capitalism in Britain and the United States: A Critical Appraisal* (London: Routledge, 1989).

# 6

# Democracy and
# Human Development

Describing what ought to be done in politics is easier than specifying how it can be accomplished. Our discussion thus far has focused on spelling out an analytic approach that would show the way to better policies. But what about the processes of governance and social decision making? How can we fit the dynamic of identity development into the procedural form of democracy so as to generate the policies that would improve the human condition? This brings us to the problem of identity and democracy, a critical issue for our era. It is now time to address this problem directly and to see if a fully worked-out concept of identity can reveal some solutions to the conflicts that undermine and frustrate the realization of democratic principles.

## Democracy as
## Social Learning

Democracy is a method for making social decisions while reserving the right to change these decisions in view of new conditions, knowledge, and perceptions. Democracy combines both the possibility of social decision making and the right of individual choice. While democracies do not attach any requirement of wisdom to the act of voting, they do, through periodic elections, allow social learning to take place.

*Democracy, at its best, may be seen as a social learning process.* Conceived of as an instrument for testing and refining the knowledge of the community, democracies can be evaluated by the canons appropriate to the examination of learning processes. In technical terms, we need to undertake, albeit briefly, an epistemological inquiry.[1]

Identity analysis is consistent with the view that learning takes place not through the revelation of divine truth, or of an absolute morality, but through the working out of relationships between individual promptings and social interactions. According to the theorists whose work we have seen to have empirical resonance, there is a structure to this learning transaction. We cannot be false to our individual talents and find a true identity. Nor can we assert a wholly idiosyncratic identity and expect that it will be ratified as a form of competence by the community.

Similarly, experience teaches us that the failure of mutuality is debilitating, just as the sustenance of it is rewarding. The assertion of a version of our place in the world that has us, or our group, in some status of exclusive privilege is bound to be undone in the test of human interaction. The interesting question is how we can translate this sort of learning to the level of a political process that will yield sensible policies that support human development.

Were we to engage in this kind of social epistemology, there would predictably be limits placed on the role of entrenched power in favor of deliberation and open procedures. There would be support for the widest possible expression of views and the clearest possible accountability for public policy decisions. There is no absolute truth in identity analysis, but there are powerful probabilities that need to be allowed to rise to the surface of social consciousness.

Given the protections for individual rights of dissent, there would also be the presumption that in decisions affecting the whole community, what the larger portion of the community has agreed to should hold for all rather than the views of a lesser portion of the community. By this test, private centers of power would be required to give way to public forms of decision making in community decisions. The justification provided here is not so much that the majority may know the truth as that, given the inevitable power of social forces over individual life, the shaping of those forces should reflect the widest possible participation of the community under conditions most likely to produce a wise application of social knowledge.

This view is meant to contrast directly with the politicized epistemology of the theorist most responsible for contemporary individualist conservative ideology, Friedrich A. Hayek.[2] His view and my own start from a similar assumption: knowledge is dispersed and particularistic in character. We reach different institutional conclusions, however. Hayek argues that only the market, as an institutionally formless vehicle for spontaneous human behavior, can make the best mobilization of knowledge in the service of human needs and aspirations.[3] What he ignores, curiously, is the corrupting influence of self-preferment on knowledge.

Self-preferment is, by its nature, particularistic and dispersed just as knowledge is, and the former is known to corrupt the latter. The purpose of democracy is to mobilize knowledge while limiting the effects of self-preferment. The double test of an argument in a properly deliberative democracy is whether it makes sense or not, and whether it is socially useful or merely self-serving.

Because democracies might well simply aggregate the self-preferring decisions of a majority at the expense of minorities, we have constitutions designed to place boundaries on such preferences, even while establishing processes that include the open pursuit and free expression of knowledge. Yet, to say that knowledge is dispersed and particularistic does not mean that it cannot be communicated, shared, and validated by communities. It is the *control* of knowledge at the community level that contains the seeds of tyranny, not the nurturing and aggregation of shared experience in a democratic society.

Hayek's market, however, contains no such restraints on self-preferment; the market combines self-preferment with a manifestly unequal distribution of resources. The individualist position is indeed merely a justification for private aggregations of power and the untrammeled ability to enforce self-preferment through the use of that power to shape social forces that affect others to their disadvantage. Far from liberating individual choice, the individualist position winds up, in the form given it by Hayek, permitting powerful individuals to suborn the less powerful through economic means with little, if any, recourse to institutional protections against exploitation.

Similarly, Hayek's political views have the effect of dismantling the means by which knowledge can be separated from self-preferment. That is, indeed, the purpose of democratic institutions, and Hayek's enterprise is to limit and restrict their power to accomplish that task. By placing the ability to affect social forces at the individual level, rather than in constitutionally bounded social decision-making processes, Hayek links the disposition of knowledge to the most powerful of all corrupters of knowledge, self-preferment. By arguing for the market and other forms of unbridled individual choice, he substitutes knowledge corrupted by self-preference for knowledge validated through democratic procedures.[4]

Socially useful knowledge of the kind we have presented here, tested against observation and experience, has a legitimacy superior to that of individual knowledge in making policy on public matters. While the latter must always be honored in the discussion of policy, progressive responses to the prevailing disposition of social forces depend on being able to mobilize insights from inquiries such as Erikson's. We must, indeed, have the institutional means of limiting self-preferment, exposing the corruption of knowledge, and acting in a manner counter to assertions of private power. It is now time to see how this works out in the case at hand. The question is, what should democratic regimes do by coercion, and what by eliciting voluntary cooperation?

## Power and Authority in Governance

At the core of politics is the existence of power in society. Coercion is only one aspect of governance, however. Governance encompasses the voluntary as well as the coercive. Legitimate authority is characterized by voluntary compliance. Democracy acquires its legitimacy through voluntary participation. A theory of politics must have a conceptual basis for understanding both the voluntary and the coercive aspects of governance. Why do we obey *voluntarily,* and under what circumstances should we be *made to obey?*

The essential distinction for these purposes is between relations of power and relations of authority. *Power* involves the ability to coerce compliance; *authority* rests on the capacity to enlist compliance voluntarily. Political systems that rely on a high level of authority have little need for exercises of power. The respected coach, the natural team leader, the dissident with integrity—all command a following that no amount of power can compel. In contrast, totalitarian systems use power and the threat of coercion to produce conformity with regime goals and work hard at producing the illusion of voluntary compliance. The emphasis on public spectacles and ceremonial displays is part of the mask that power wears.

The voluntary aspect of politics is the more neglected. Following on what has been determined about the centrality of identity, voluntary compliance arises when social processes offer the validation of competence, the enhancement of one's sense of purpose and meaning, and the nurturance of relationships of mutuality. To the extent that these are natural processes of development, the cultivation of voluntary support for the authority of the community depends upon building up these possibilities.

An analysis based on human development tells us how to distinguish legitimate from illegitimate authority. Authority arises from the ability to lead the way toward the fulfillment of some crucial aspiration, including higher forms of human development. That is why *competent* people are respected, as are those who have a sensible and integrated view of themselves and the world, and those who have demonstrated the ability to sustain commitments. As a community, we honor these people by promotions to new responsibilities, awards for service, commemorations of anniversaries, and everyday forms of deference and respect.

While there are authorities among criminals, and heroes and heroines in gangs, the dividing line between legitimate and illegitimate authority lies along the fault lines of human development. Those forms of authority based on the achievement of developmental strength are legitimized in society as meritorious;

authorities that exploit confusion and despair without offering useful solutions have a limited tenure.

A society that is truly democratic offers a multitude of arenas where authority may be earned. The meaning of freedom of expression as a critical ingredient of democracy is, in addition to its contribution to the dynamism of knowledge, that expression provides the information on which assessments of authority are based. Only a free expression of ideas can expose the falseness of claims by would-be authorities and make possible the delegitimation of fraudulent appeals to basic human aspirations.

The exhilaration of solidarity flows from the affirmation that social processes offer for the crucial aspirations of the psyche. In the affirmative mode, political processes offer the transactional medium for progressive action to address basic human needs, to inspire common action, and to overcome great obstacles. Within its institutional forms, affirmative politics enables individuals to find sources of meaning, the tangible methods of developing and demonstrating competence, and the organizational continuity that makes committed relationships possible.

To protect against violations of freedom of expression, and to recognize the primacy of individual dignity, is to acknowledge the nature of human development. The case for permitting self-expression is based not just in a moral abstraction about the desirability of free choice, as with Friedrich Hayek and Milton Friedman, but rather in a substantive understanding of human development.[5]

Identity cannot be provided by an act of public policy. It is an internal achievement that can be facilitated or hampered by social processes. The assembly of meanings that make an identity must be harmonized by the individual. Expressive freedom is required to allow this to happen.

## Coercion and the Pathologies of Identity

Not all of politics is affirmative, however. As Erikson demonstrates, the processes of identity formation and defense have about them a negative side. There is a pathology of identity formation that arises from discrimination and chauvinism. By the denigration of differences among categories of people, false superiorities can be asserted. The scale of behavior that follows from pseudospeciation runs from discrimination to genocide. This pathology provides a guideline for understanding negative politics, and, with it, the role of power and coercion in a properly constructed polity.

*The principal purpose of coercion in politics should be to limit the effects of pathologies in identity formation.* The main form taken by identity as pathology is domination. Murder is the ultimate manifestation of interindividual domination; rape is another; and the violation of basic rights of self-expression is a broader manifestation. Child sexual abuse is, for example, highly correlated with just about every significant social malady. Just as there is a common interest in avoiding these manifestations, there is a legitimate pretext for political processes that use force, if necessary, to prevent them from happening.

While coercion has a role in safeguarding essential developmental freedoms, affirmative politics offers the possibility of more creative solutions to developmental challenges. The least burdensome threshold of justification for a community's action involves creating sensible developmental options that can be freely chosen by its members. *The function of government in relation to human development is primarily to create choices rather than to compel conformity.* I have specified here a starting point for investigating what those choices need to be.

# Democracy: Participation for the Sake of Human Development

The first consideration has to be democracy as a political method. A fully developed concept of identity allows for a distinction in participation between those forms that support the process of human development and those forms, such as domination and discrimination, that degrade and destroy developmental possibilities. The *intent* of participation is as important as the form if democracy is to become something other than a passive procedure, or a plebiscite for authority.

Inclusiveness as a goal in political participation is obviously to be desired. Nevertheless, forms of inclusiveness that equalize participation without building up competence in making policy decisions run the risk of a kind of reverse domination.[6] The least informed, least public-spirited elements of the group can exercise a veto that stymies the possibility of constructive policy.

Similarly, participative processes need to incorporate means of communication that facilitate exchanges whereby differing visions can be expressed of the integrative principles that tie communities together. These principles can make it possible for individuals to bring into balance the particular and universal aspects of their own strivings for identity. Some of the greatest abuses of democracy in this century have been systems that are inclusive in the plebiscitary sense only—where everyone has a voice, but the voice can only say yes or no to the leader. The analogue is public opinion polls that ask yes or no questions on taxation without regard to fiscal realities. The latter may provide some kind of useful information but no realistic participation in effective decision making.

Particularist approaches in the name of identity politics can likewise threaten democracy. Where there is only the demand for "voice" without any consideration for shared values or common needs, there is the potential for rising levels of insecurity and the fragmentation of community. Identity in its social dimension is an interactive process. Assertions of worth that are not grounded in shared values lead to counterassertions from threatened groups. At the same time, to ignore differences is also damaging to democracy. As Susan Mendus points out in an essay on "Feminism and Democracy":

> For whereas traditional democratic theory tends to construe difference as an obstacle to the attainment of a truly democratic state, feminist theory should alert us to the possibility that difference is rather what necessitates the pursuit of democracy. Since it is the fact that we are not all the same which requires democracy, attempting to make us all the same will not deliver democracy. On the contrary, it will remove the rationale for democracy.[7]

Democracy may be seen as the method that allows, on a basis of equal rights of participation, the aggregation of social learning even as it accommodates differences between individuals and groups. The market creates presumptions of superiority and inferiority by virtue of wealth; democracies theoretically operate without such presumptions, especially when the role of money in politics is sharply curtailed. While the failure to differentiate among its citizens may be seen by some theorists as a denial of legitimate distinctions, ultimately the best assurance that minorities may avoid persecution lies in a universalist approach to democracy. As Mendus indicates, the *politics* of democracy exists to accommodate the distributed and particularistic aspects of the human condition, but the universalist framework within which these differences are accommodated exists as the final protection of difference itself.

The concept of identity advanced here suggests that the building of respect on the basis of various kinds of competence, contributions to the integrative purposes of the community, and the demonstration of mutual commitment and sustained effort at progressive reform are the building blocks for a lasting recognition of diversity.

Participation has an explicitly qualitative dimension. The forms of participation that foster mutuality and the inculcation of a shared sense of responsibility are essential aspects of democracy. A state that is run as if it were a shopping mall where many gather solely for the purpose of individual self-interest will not survive very long. Democratic traditions that institutionalize accountability, responsibility for collective decisions, and the careful development of leadership make possible the governing of large, complex communities. Various kinds of partnerships, cooperatives, and profit-sharing plans serve the purposes of democracy in smaller associations.

# Public Policy:
# Ventures in Human Development

The next consideration involves the content of public policy. Illustrative policies can be specified that support trust, autonomy, initiative, industry, intimacy, generativity, and integrity—the developmental benchmarks of Erikson's life stages. Similarly, it is possible to point to policies that foster mistrust, shame, guilt, inferiority, isolation, stagnation, and despair. By recasting policy discussions in these terms, we can see that the distinction between state action and individual action is, in part, misleading. The essential distinction is between benign developmental possibilities and the foreclosure of development.

To refuse to formulate a coherent community response to essential aspects of development is not the same as enabling the individual to make a "free" choice in the matter. Education, along with welfare and employment policies, can be rationalized according to its contribution to human development. To create "equal opportunity" for someone with neither the skills for a decent job nor the prospect of obtaining them is to engage in a hollow exercise. To permit the unregulated disposition of pension funds, and other instruments by which individuals can provide for their own security and that of their families, is to undercut the developmental basis of mutual commitment.

The assault on nondemocratic practices is, by the logic of human development, a matter of many actions across a broad front. Distinctions between public and private power, and between individual self-interest and the public interest, are less relevant in this view than the reinforcement of constructive forms of participation in every sphere of life. At the same time, the use of state authority and power to protect against abuses of developmental processes is an essential, if sensitive and complicated, task that undergirds the evolution of democracy.

While it is beyond the scope of this book to suggest more specific policies, it is the purpose here to sketch some of the conceptual frameworks within which these policies can be developed. Historically, democracy arrives either as a result of the collapse of authoritarianism and/or as the evolutionary result of experiments over time. The imposition of simple models of procedural democracy will not succeed without a broad-scale advance in forms of democratic behavior that sustain and enhance processes of human development. Of these, the intricate dynamics of identity formation and defense must be of primary concern.

In the end, we return to the birth of democracy. As Cynthia Farrar reminds us, in Athenian society, "justice is legitimated if it is shown to be essential to personal well-being. Athenian political life raised the possibility of maintaining a bracing tension between personal and civic identity."[8] The democratization of nondemocratic societies requires that this tension be worked through in all spheres of society: the state, the market, and the civil society. The first step is to understand the nature of the tension.

## Notes

1. Cf. Benjamin Barber, *The Aristocracy of Everyone: The Politics of Education and the Future of America* (New York: Ballantine Books, 1992).

2. Hayek prefers not to be labeled a conservative, which he identifies with traditionalist opposition to change, but rather a "classical liberal." Nevertheless, the tendency of all his ideas is toward the defense of inequalities and distinctions among people, which is the reverse of the intent of classical liberalism. John Locke, Jeremy Bentham, John Stuart Mill, and even Adam Smith were, both in the historical context of their times and in the applications of their ideas, arguing for forms of political economy that validated claims to an equality of rights and of political/economic opportunity, if not of result. Cf. Friedrich Hayek, "Why I Am Not a Conservative [1960]," in Chiaki Nishiyama and Kurt Leube, *The Essence of Hayek* (Palo Alto, Calif.: Stanford University/Hoover Institution Press, 1984), 281–98; cf. Hayek, *The Constitution of Liberty* (Chicago: University of Chicago Press, 1960), 24. The position taken here is that conservatism is of two minds: traditionalist and, more contemporarily, "individualist." See Kenneth R. Hoover, "Conservatism," in *The Routledge Encyclopedia of Government and Politics*, ed. Maurice Kogan and Mary Hawkesworth (London: Routledge, 1992), 139–54.

3. Friedrich Hayek, "The Principles of a Liberal Social Order [1967]," in Nishiyama and Leube, *The Essence of Hayek*, 367–68; and idem, "The Origins and Effects of Our Morals: A Problem for Science [1983]," in ibid., 318–30.

4. Hayek argues that government is somehow the captive of reason and that rationality is only part of knowledge, the better to leave decisions to individuals in such formations as the market. There is, of course, nothing about democracy that compels citizens to make choices only on the basis of reason other than the attraction that rea-

son validated by experience might have—and the observed consequences of irrationality. In this way, a constitutional democracy is every bit as much a device for learning wisdom as the market is. Cf. Hayek, *Constitution of Liberty*, 64, 70.

5. Kenneth Hoover and Raymond Plant, *Conservative Capitalism in Britain and the United States: A Critical Appraisal* (London: Routledge, 1989), chap. 11.

6. Cynthia Farrar, "Ancient Greek Political Theory as a Response to Democracy," in *Democracy: The Unfinished Journey 508 B.C. to A.D. 1993*, ed. John Dunn (New York: Oxford University Press, 1992), 38.

7. Susan Mendus, "Losing the Faith: Feminism and Democracy," in Dunn, *Democracy: The Unfinished Journey*, 216.

8. Farrar, "Ancient Greek Political Theory," 17.

## PART TWO

# Identity and Politics: Evidence and Application

# 7

# Ego Identity:
# Research Review
## by James Marcia

Identity status research has spanned more than twenty-five years and more than 300 studies. Although not all are reviewed in this chapter, the ones that are covered give a fairly coherent picture of what has been determined with some certainty and what is questionable. The issues raised in the four extensive reviews of identity status research (Bourne 1978a, b; Marcia 1980; Matteson 1975; and Waterman 1982) suggest the structure for this chapter, which is divided into four sections: (1) personality characteristics of the different identity statuses, emphasizing "the internalization of self-regulatory processes"; (2) developmental aspects; (3) gender differences and sex roles; and (4) cross-cultural studies.

## Personality Characteristics
## of the Identity Statuses: The Internalization
## of Self-Regulatory Processes

"Internalization" is a concept shared by these theories: drive-oriented classical psychoanalytic, adaptation-oriented ego psy-

*Note:* This chapter presents a summary of the work of numerous researchers who have done empirical studies of Erikson's concept of identity. It is reprinted with permission from J.E. Marcia, "The Status of the

choanalytic, relationship-oriented object relations, and cognitive developmental. Bourne (1978b) writes from a psychoanalytic perspective:

> This process involves the development of an increasingly stabilized and internalized capacity for ... homeostatic control of internal functioning, particularly in the realms of (1) the regulation of self-esteem (Kohut 1971), (2) the exercise of self-calming functions and containment of affective fluctuations in response to stress, and (3) the autonomous organization of motives and resources to anticipate and meet adaptive demands. (Blos 1974, 89)

Similarly, both Piaget's (1965) stages of cognitive development and Kohlberg's (1976) stages in the development of moral thought involve progressive internalization, self-representation, and self-construction of the world and of values.

The personality variables discussed in this section have in common an emphasis on an internal (structurally mature) mode of control and valuation contrasted with an external (structurally immature) mode. These are the general patterns expected from the identity statuses: Identity Diffusions should be the least internalized; having no firm identity, they are defined by their circumstances. Foreclosures may appear to be more internalized than Moratoriums; however, their internalization is based upon introjected, unreconstructed authority figures, and reflects little "metabolism" or sophisticated syntheses of early identifications—life issues have not been reformulated in the individual's own terms. Moratoriums, who are in the process of synthesizing internal structures may, in times of crisis, appear less internalized than Foreclosures; in less acute periods they should appear more internalized than Foreclosures, and they should always appear more internalized than Diffusions. Identity Achievement persons, having constructed their own identities, should appear to be the most internalized of the statuses.

---

Statuses: Research Review," in *Ego Identity: A Handbook for Research,* ed. J.E. Marcia, A.S. Waterman, D.R. Matteson, S.L. Archer, and J.L. Orlofsky (New York: Springer-Verlag, 1993).

# General Personality Characteristics

## Authoritarianism and Stereotypical Thinking

One of the most consistent findings in identity status research has been that male and female Foreclosures, especially relative to Moratoriums, score highly on measures of authoritarianism and socially stereotypical thinking (Marcia 1966, 1967; Marcia and Friedman 1970; Matteson 1974; Schenkel and Marcia 1972; and Streitmatter and Pate 1989). They show preference for a strong leader over a democratic process, obedience over social protest, and the "pseudospeciation" described by Erikson (1987): firm conviction that "their" group and "their" way are right. A possible consequence of this position is the somewhat chilling finding by Podd (1972) that, more than any other group in a Milgram obedience task who had delivered what they believed to be maximum electrical shock to a "victim," it was the Foreclosures who were willing to do it again; in fact, all Foreclosures who administered maximum shock levels were willing to repeat their performance.

## Anxiety

The ability to bind anxiety, to perform effectively in the face of inner turmoil, is a characteristic associated with higher levels of ego functioning, such as would ensue from formation of an identity. One caution about interpreting studies of anxiety among the identity statuses is that most of these have used paper-and-pencil self-report measures, which yield the estimate of anxiety that a subject is willing to report. In general, Moratoriums and, to a lesser extent, Diffusions have been highest in reported anxiety among the statuses, and Foreclosures have been the lowest (Marcia 1967; Marcia and Friedman 1970; Oshman and Manosevitz 1974; Podd et al. 1970; and Sterling and Van Horn 1989). The differences in identity statuses' reported anxiety are likely to be obtained for differing reasons. Moratoriums score highly because they are in a stressful, in-crisis state, and because they tend to be excruciatingly honest. Foreclosures may score low both because it may be a particularly adaptive status in some groups in certain historical periods, and because they are reluctant to admit pathology. The latter is reflected in their high social desirability scores (Orlofsky et al. 1973).

## Self-Esteem

Although differences among statuses in stability of self-esteem were established in early studies, findings have not been clear on absolute levels of self-esteem. For example, Marcia (1967) and Orlofsky (1977) found no self-esteem differences in males; but Bunt (1968) found high identity males to be high in self-esteem. Foreclosure* and Achievement women had higher self-esteem than Moratorium and Diffusion women, according to Marcia and Friedman (1970) and Schenkel and Marcia (1972); but Prager (1982) and Read et al. (1984) found that only Identity Achievement women had high self-esteem scores; and Orlofsky (1977) reported no differences among women. One problem in this research area is the differing theoretical definitions of self-esteem. Within the ego psychoanalytic theoretical context of the identity statuses, self-esteem ought to refer to the similarity experienced between one's personal attributes and one's ego ideal standards, a match that should improve in adolescence as the unrealistically high goals of childhood introjects are modified (Blos 1962; Josselson 1980; Marcia 1983). The identity formation process of questioning, exploration, and commitment is central to this modification. Foreclosures, who have not undergone the differentiation process, should have unrealistically high ego ideals and correspondingly low self-esteem. Identity Achievement persons should have a more realistically reconstructed ego ideal and higher resultant self-esteem. Some evidence for this description was found in Foreclosures' tendency to maintain and even raise their goals in the face of failures on a concept attainment task (Marcia 1966) and their tendency toward underachievement (Berzonsky 1985; Hummel and Roselli 1983; Streitmatter 1989). However, a definitive answer to the

---

* On a number of variables, an Achievement-Foreclosure grouping women contrasted with the expected Achievement-Moratorium grouping. This result seems due to social-historical factors described in the Gender Differences section of this chapter.

identity-self-esteem relationship awaits the construction of a more theoretically relevant measure.

# Independence of External Pressure
## Locus of Control

Locus of control refers to one's assignment of responsibility for what befalls oneself either to an external (luck, fate) or an internal source (Rotter 1966). Because they have undergone a self-constructive identity formation process, individuals high in identity (Achievements and Moratoriums) are expected to be more internal, and Foreclosures and Diffusions are expected to have a more external orientation. These results were found for men (C.K. Waterman et al. 1970), for women (Howard 1975), and for men and women (Dellas and Jernigan 1987). Matteson (1974), studying Danish youths, found no differences on this variable. Ginsburg and Orlofsky (1981) and Grossman, Shea, and Adams (1980) found Achievement and Foreclosure women to be somewhat more internal than the other statuses. Matteson (personal communication) suggests that the Foreclosures' apparent internal orientation reported here may be due to socially desirable responding. In summary, Achievements tend to have an internal locus of control and Diffusions are external; the placement of Moratoriums and Foreclosures is intermediate, and their relative positions are variable.

## Autonomy

Studying autonomy and self-directedness in males, Orlofsky et al. (1973) found Foreclosures to be lowest, and Matteson (1974) found both Foreclosures and Diffusions to be low. Similarly, C.K. Waterman and Waterman (1975) and Waterman and Goldman (1976) described Foreclosure men as reliant on their families for making life decisions, and Andrews (1973) reported male subjects high in identity to be independent and achieving, contrasted with low identity subjects' more passive, affective stance. Chapman and Nicholls (1976), studying New Zealand boys, reported the highest field independence among Achievements. Schenkel (1975) found Identity Achievement and Foreclosure women to be the most field independent of the statuses.

Among men, then, it appears that Foreclosures and Diffusions are the least autonomous, but among women there is evidence for a high autonomy pattern for both Achievements and Foreclosures.

### Change in Self-Esteem and Conformity

A direct way of looking at resistance to external pressure is to create social pressure experimentally and observe performance. This experiment was done in the first studies by Marcia (1966, 1967), described in chapter 1 of Marcia et al. (1993). Toder and Marcia (1973), studying conformity in college women using an Asch type of task, demonstrated that Achievement persons conformed less and felt less discomfort than individuals in the other statuses. Foreclosure, not Moratorium, women were similar in their nonconformity to Achievements. Adams et al. (1984), though not directly replicating the Marcia and Toder study, did find among college men and women a greater tendency for Diffusions than for the other statuses to conform on a social peer-pressure measure. In summary, Identity Achievement individuals seem resistant to external pressures, and Diffusions are more compliant.

## Ego Development

Loevinger and Wessler's (1970) measure of ego development describes progressively differentiated levels of "frameworks of meaning which one subjectively imposes on experience" (Hauser 1976, 930). Individuals are categorized according to three levels of ego organization: Pre-Conformist (impulsive to self-protective); Conformist (conformist to conscientious); and Post-Conformist (autonomous to integrative). Contrasted with Erikson's psychosocial scheme, Loevinger's ego developmental theory is more general, refers more to underlying psychological structure, and is less specifically related to life-cycle stages. Loevinger's and Erikson's developmental notions have in common Werner's (1957) proposals of progressive differentiation, internalization, and hierarchical integration of ego functions.

The hypothesis that a certain level of ego development may

be a necessary condition for identity formation and that this successful resolution should then contribute to further ego development was tested by Adams and Fitch (1981, 1982) in both cross-lag and cross-sequential design studies. Although they found a significant positive relationship between the two constructs, they were unable to demonstrate any causal connections. Another study confirming this relationship was that of Adams and Shea (1979), who found that among college males and females Achievements were at higher levels of ego development, that they were the only identity status present at the highest Post-Conformist (integrated) level, and that they never fell below the autonomous level. Also, Ginsburg and Orlofsky (1981), in a study of college women, found that Achievements and Moratoriums were located more frequently in the Post-Conformist stages, but Foreclosures and Diffusions tended to be Conformist and Pre-Conformist. Newman (1986), studying young noncollege women in an urban shelter, found a significant relationship between overall identity development and Loevinger's ego development. In summary, a positive relationship between identity status and ego development is well established; the exact nature of the relationship between the two and between the ego developmental stages and the psychosocial stages in general remains to be explored.

One behavioral area in which to observe effects of ego development is impulse control—specifically substance abuse. An investigation of nonprescription drug use in college showed that Foreclosures were predominant in, and Moratoriums notably absent from, the category of "adamant non-drug-user" (Dufresne and Cross 1972), a finding consistent with Matteson's (1978) description of Danish Identity Achievement and Moratorium youths as freer in impulse expression than Foreclosures. Pack et al. (1976) reported a relationship between identity commitment (Achievement and Foreclosure) and the ability to stop using marijuana. Jones and Hartmann (1988), investigating the relationship between drug use and identity development in high school students, found Diffuse persons to be the most frequent users, Foreclosures least frequent, and Achievements and Moratoriums intermediate.

# Cognitive Performance and Cognitive Style

An increment to ego strength in the form of a positive resolution of a psychosocial developmental stage such as identity should positively affect primary ego functions such as ability to think and plan. Hence, it was thought that the identity statuses should differ in measures of cognitive performance. A necessary precondition for investigating this relationship was the establishment of no significant differences among the identity statuses in general intelligence (Bob 1968; Cross and Allen 1970; Marcia 1966; Marcia and Friedman 1970; Schenkel 1975).

After Marcia's (1966) initial findings of a positive relationship between identity and cognitive performance under stress, Bob (1968), also studying college males, stated that as a cognitive task became more difficult, Foreclosures became cognitively constricted and Diffusions tended to withdraw. Waterman and Waterman (1972) found that Identity Achievement college students had better study habits than other statuses; unsurprisingly, Cross and Allen (1970) found them to have higher gradepoint averages, and, finally, in an initial study on women's identity development, Marcia and Friedman (1970) reported that Achievements chose the most difficult, and Diffusions the least difficult, college majors. Similarly, studying high school girls, Raphael (1977) reported that Achievements had the highest gradepoint averages.

Perhaps a more important issue than cognitive performance is cognitive style, the way in which one approaches cognitive tasks. One variable is the degree of complexity a person displays. Côté and Reker (1979) found that among college men, the "unstable" statuses of Diffusion and Moratorium had more complex cognitive systems than did the "stable" Achievement status. (There were no Foreclosures in this study.) Likewise, Kirby (1977) found Foreclosures to be cognitively simple and Diffusions more complex. Tzuriel and Klein (1977), studying Israeli settlers, reported a curvilinear relationship between identity and complexity: high identity associated with moderate complexity; low identity was related to either high or low complexity. Extrapolating somewhat from these three studies, it appears that Achievements and Moratoriums are relatively complex cognitively; Foreclosures are relatively simple cognitively; and Diffusions are extremely complex, some of them, perhaps, disorganized. Attempting to be more precise about the issue of cognitive approach, Berzonsky and Niemeyer (1988), using Kelly's (1955) Role Repertory Grid, have identified different information-processing styles among the identity statuses (e.g., Achievements as information-oriented and self-exploring, Foreclosures as normative, and Diffusions as diffuse and ad hoc).*

Another aspect of cognitive style is an attribute that could be described as thoughtfulness or creativity, one's ability and willingness to go beneath the surface of things and perhaps to come up with new ideas or syntheses. The following studies considered this depth or openness quality of cognitive style. Waterman et al. (1974) and Waterman and Goldman (1976) reported that college students high in identity were more culturally sophisticated than those low in identity; and Waterman et al. (1977) and Waterman and Archer (1979) found that high identity males and females in high school and college were more frequent poetry writers than low identity persons. This tendency for high identity persons to be more creative has been attributed by Gombosi (1972) and by Bilsker and Marcia (1991) to their capacity for adaptive regression. Studying college males, C.K. Waterman and Waterman (1974) reported that Achievement and Moratorium persons, compared with Foreclosures and Diffusions, were more reflective than impulsive; a finding replicated by Shain and Farber (1989) studying college women. Finally, Tesch and Cameron (1987), extending the study of identity development into young adulthood, remarked that openness to experience correlated positively with identity exploration (Moratorium-like) and negatively with intense commitment (Foreclosure-like).

---

* Recently, a very promising research area concerning decision-making information-processing styles characteristic of the identity statuses has expanded considerably (Berzonsky 1985, 1989, 1990); Berzonsky, Rice, and Niemeyer 1990; Berzonsky and Sullivan, 1992; Blustein and Phillips 1990; Neimeyer and Rareshide 1991).

# Formal Operational Thinking and Identity Development

The possibility that attaining formal operational thought is either a condition necessary for, or an accompaniment of, identity resolution has been suggested by Chandler (1987), Erikson (1952), Marcia (1980), and Kohlberg and Gilligan (1972), who stated: "... the relativistic questioning of conventional morality and conventional reality associated with logical development is also central to the adolescent's identity concerns" (p. 171). On the other hand, Blasi and Hoeffel (1974) have argued persuasively against this position; they are supported by Berzonsky and Barclay (1981) and Kurfiss (1981).

The preponderance of evidence supports an intermediate position. Wagner (1987), studying college males and females, found a positive relationship between one of two measures of formal operations and one of two measures of identity. Rowe and Marcia (1980) obtained a positive relationship between identity and formal operations with college males and females; however, their study included only three Achievements. Finally, Leadbetter and Dionne (1981) reported a positive relationship between the two variables among male high school students. Among those who have failed to confirm such a relationship are Afrifah (1980), Berzonsky et al. (1975), Cauble (1976), and Leiper (1981). Clearly, the strong case for the identity-formal operations relationship, that the latter is a necessary condition for the former, cannot be supported.

As one moves from physical-mathematical indices of formal operational thought to social-moral ones, the picture changes. Using a broader, more socially oriented measure of cognitive sophistication, integrative complexity, Slugoski et al. (1984) found that, among college males, Achievements and Moratoriums were clearly more cognitively advanced than Foreclosures and Diffusions, with Moratoriums scoring higher than Achievements. Boyes and Chandler (1992), employing a measure of levels of skeptical doubt, found that high identity high school students were at more sophisticated levels than low identity students.

In the development of moral thought, assumed to depend on

levels of cognitive development (Kohlberg 1976), the theoretical link with identity is clear and the empirical relationship is well established. Both identity and moral reasoning are assumed to involve the cognitive developmental processes of disequilibration (questioning, exploration) and accommodation (resolution, commitment). Only one study (Cauble 1976) has not found a relationship between identity and levels of moral reasoning. Among those who have demonstrated this relationship are Lieper (1981) and Podd (1972) with college males; Hult (1979) and Poppen (1974) with women; and Rowe and Marcia (1980) with college men and women. Interestingly, as in the Slugoski et al. (1984) study, Moratoriums frequently score higher than Achievements. Skoe and Marcia (1991) have extended these findings to include the establishment of a relationship between identity in women and "care-based" moral developmental thought as described by Carol Gilligan (1982). Among these college women, the relationship between the care-based measure and identity was greater than was that between the justice-based measure and identity.

Using non-Piagetian measures of moral development, Hogan (1973) found high identity individuals to be more empathic, ethical, and socialized than low identity persons. Simmons using the IAS (see chapter 1 of Marcia et al. 1993) reported that persons high in identity were more compassionate and had a more balanced concern both for their own freedom and for the well-being of others than did low identity persons.

## Interactive Styles

The foregoing sections dealt primarily with those personality characteristics of the identity statuses reflecting internalization of self-regulatory processes. This portion reviews studies describing the ways in which different identity status individuals interact with their peers and how they are perceived by them.

In a study of patterns of cooperation and competition in a Prisoner's Dilemma game, Podd et al. (1970) reported that Moratoriums emerged as the distinctive group, displaying less cooperation with an authority opponent than with a peer, yet matching their opponents' responses more than the other statuses

—seen as a Moratorium tendency toward both rebellion and conformity. Adams et al. (1987) wrote that adolescents in the higher identity statuses were less self-conscious than those in lower statuses. Read et al. (1984), studying identity status and social influence style among college women, found that Foreclosure women perceived themselves as less analytic, less philosophical, and less able to integrate ideas from multiple perspectives. Behaviorally, they were the most interpersonally manipulative (least self-revealing), and, together with Diffusions, most likely to use bribes and deception to exert social influence. Achievement and Moratorium women said that they enjoyed being alone with their own thoughts and that they were able to process extensive stimulus information. Interacting with others, they used more direct, assertive social influence techniques, thus risking social disapproval. Among college men, Slugoski et al. (1984) stated that Foreclosures displayed two predominant styles in small-group discussions of moral issues: aggressive assertion or submissive compliance. Both strategies were viewed as their defenses against changing preformed opinions. Clinical psychology graduate students who were Identity Achievements were found to have more facilitating counseling styles than non-Achievements (Genthner and Neuber 1975; Neuber and Genthner 1977). Finally, Goldman et al. (1980) solicited reactions to persons described according to their identity status. Achievements and Moratoriums were most liked, and seen as intelligent, knowledgeable, and well adjusted. (Men also reported more satisfaction with peer support in a study by Caldwell et al. 1989). Diffusions were least liked, and generally evaluated lowest. Subjects who were themselves non-Diffusions preferred identity-committed targets, but Diffusions preferred noncommitted targets. The authors wrote: "If you have undergone a crisis you are judged by all as being more likeable, intelligent, knowledgeable, and adjusted" (p. 161).

Two persons have completed noteworthy descriptive studies of identity statuses' interactional style: James Donovan (1970, 1975) and Ruthellen Josselson (1972, 1973, 1988). Both investigators used the results of a number of psychodynamic-based measures as well as classroom and interview observations to describe their subjects. Because no brief summary could do justice to the richness of these descriptive presentations, we recommend the original material. Of special interest is Josselson's (1988) book describing, longitudinally, women's pathways of identity development, with much-needed emphasis on the connection as well as the separation component of individuation.

## Developmental Aspects of the Identity Statuses

The greatest volume of research since Marcia's (1980) literature review has considered developmental issues, and a chapter in Marcia et al. (1993) is devoted to this subject. It is to be expected that, in the course of establishing construct validity, once concurrent and predictive validity are ascertained, antecedent and consequent conditions can be determined.

Two studies investigating age boundaries of initial identity resolution are those of Meilman (1979) and Archer (1982). Meilman, studying males in age groups from twelve to twenty-four found no Achievements or Moratoriums among twelve-year-olds and only 4 percent among fifteen-year-olds. The appearance of significant numbers of Achievements and Moratoriums began at age eighteen and increased until age twenty-four, with a corresponding decrease in Foreclosures and Diffusions throughout this age span. The most noticeable change from lower to higher identity statuses occurred around age 21–22. Archer investigated change in identity status in specific interview domains among eleven- to seventeen-year-old boys and girls. She found 19 percent Achievements and Moratoriums among seventeen-year-olds, corresponding closely to Meilman's 24 percent among eighteen-year-olds. The occupational domain was the area in which most junior and senior high school students were Identity Achieved. Raphael (1975) reported no high school senior females in the Identity Achievement status. The conclusion that may be drawn from these studies is that when the overall identity status category system is used, Moratoriums and Achievements do not appear much before the senior year in high school, although persons may be high in identity in specific domains. Also, if one uses a continuous scale of identity development such as the EOM-EIS (see Marcia et al., 1993, chap. 1), scores can be obtained for all statuses beginning in junior high school (see, e.g., Jones and Streitmatter 1987; Streitmatter 1989). Matteson (personal communication) states that the age boundaries cited above might not hold across socioeconomic settings (e.g., in areas where future college attendance was not a reasonable expectation).

## Childhood Antecedents

The relationship between identity formation at late adolescence and the resolution of prior psychosocial stages has been the subject of a number of studies, most of them using either Constantinople's (1969) or Rasmussen's (1964) measure. In general, positive relationships have been found between earlier stage resolution and subsequent identity formation with Identity Achievements showing most, and Diffusions showing the fewest, positive resolutions of previous stages (Waterman 1982).

Contrasting with the psychosocial approach are the studies of several researchers who have investigated more psychoanalytic-based concepts. Josselson (1982) found that Moratorium and Achievement women reported early memories at the highest psychosexual developmental level (postoedipal and blended memories) and that Foreclosures and Diffusions reported memories at lower levels (preoedipal and oedipal). These findings were replicated in a study with an improved design by Orlofsky and Frank (1986), who reported that among college males and females, Achievements and Moratoriums again had more blended or integrated (early plus later psychosexual stage) memory content than did Foreclosures and Diffusions. Early memories in both of these studies were treated as salient life-organizing themes, not as veridical accounts of events. Orlofsky and Frank's conclusion, that "mature identity resolution during late adolescence may be hindered by lack of resolution ... of basic issues of nurturance and security" (p. 20), was echoed in two studies by Kroger on attachment style among the identity statuses (1985, 1988). Attachment style refers to the nature of resolution of the separation individuation phase of early childhood development as described by Bowlby (1969) and Mahler et al.

(1975). Studying male and female college students in New Zealand, Kroger found high identity persons to be more secure and less anxiously attached than those in low identity statuses, and that the identity attachment relationship was, in general, maintained over a two-year period. Interpreting Early Memory findings as reflecting ego structuralization in adolescence, Kroger (1990) supported the results of Josselson and Orlofsky and Frank. She found that Achievements' themes involved moving alone contentedly or alongside others; Moratoriums spoke of moving against others. Foreclosures sought security and support; and Diffusions' themes were marked by a desire for relatedness.

# Middle and Late Adolescence
## Family Characteristics

Family studies on identity statuses have not been longitudinal; rather they have consisted of current perceptions of past and present family interactions, or direct measures of present family interactions; hence, it is difficult to make valid causal statements. Bearing this caveat in mind, we summarize how individuals in different identity statuses characterize their families (see Marcia 1980; Waterman 1982; and Marcia et al. 1993, chap. 3).

Foreclosures report their families as close, loving, and child-centered, with encouragement to conform to family values. Diffusions see their families as somewhat distant and rejecting; in particular, they see their same-sexed parent (whom they may admire greatly [Cella et al. 1987]) as nonaccepting and nonemulatable. Moratoriums are ambivalent about their parents and are engaged in push-pull oedipal battles, attempting to please while struggling for autonomy. Achievements have families who support their differentiation and with whom they can maintain rapprochement; the ambivalence of the Moratorium period seems to have given way to mutuality, to a balanced and realistic appraisal of similarities and differences, likes and dislikes.

Two noteworthy findings on parent variables pertain to the father's role in identity development and the equivocal effects of parental separation and absence. Father variables seem especially important in identity formation for both males and females (Bary 1978; Enright et al. 1980; Kendis and Tan 1978; LaVoie 1976). This finding bears somewhat on the importance of masculine values for identity formation (see the Sex Roles portion of this chapter). On parental separation, early studies showed that father absence (Oshman and Manosevitz 1974) and broken homes (Jordan 1970) were related to Identity Diffusion. More recent research suggests, however, that for high school girls high identity is positively related to being in a single-parent home (St. Clair and Day 1979), and among college males is associated with parental divorce (Grossman et al. 1980). The effects of parental separation on identity formation are not simple, and specific determination is likely to involve research as complex as that undertaken by Grotevant and Cooper.

These investigators, studying patterns of family interaction and their effects on adolescent identity formation via a direct, observational method, have contributed the following insights into identity formation: (1) both connectedness to and separateness from family (individuation) are important (see also Kamptner 1988); (2) differentiation between father and mother contributes to successful identity development of offspring; and (3) father-son interaction is important for boys' identity, and all family interactions are important for girls' identity (Cooper et al. 1983; Grotevant and Cooper 1983, 1985, 1986). In partial support of these findings, Campbell et al. (1984) reported that Diffusions were least attached to parents; among Achievements and Moratoriums, mother factors (especially a moderate level of affection) were important for connectedness, and father factors (especially reasonable independence from) were important for individuality (see also Papini et al. 1989); and, finally, high connectedness and low independence characterized Foreclosures, but low connectedness and moderate or low independence was characteristic of Diffusions. Similarly, in an observational study in Holland, Bosma and Gerrits (1985) reported that Achievement adolescents and their families discussed issues more actively than did Foreclosure and Diffusion families, supporting an earlier finding of Matteson's (1974) in Denmark that Achievements, contrasted with Foreclosures and Diffusions, were more nearly equal participants in family decision making. Finally, Adams (1985) reported a positive relationship between parents' and daughters' identity status, interpreting it within a pro social-learning, symbolic-interactionist framework.

## College

For three reasons, many identity status studies have used college populations: most researchers work in university settings; the age of identity resolution, around 18–22, is the age of most college students; and college is a definable social institution within which identity formation may be expected to take place. Seven longitudinal studies of identity development in college have been carried out (Adams and Fitch 1982; Costa and Campos 1988; Dellas and Jernigan 1987; Kroger 1988; Kroger and Haslett 1987; Waterman et al. 1974; Waterman and Goldman 1976). These studies are discussed in more detail in the chapter on development in Marcia et al. (1993). Very general conclusions are that Moratoriums tend to be the most unstable status (except in the Dellas and Jernigan study) and most of them become Identity Achievement in their later college years. About 50 percent of subjects change their identity status from the freshman to the senior year, the general direction being toward the higher identity statuses. In addition, there is a strong suggestion from the majority of these researchers, following the initial emphasis on this point by Waterman, that longitudinal investigations of identity development proceed by separate domains, rather than by overall identity status.

The effects of college environment on identity development have been examined in two studies. Adams and Fitch (1983) reported committed (Achievement and Foreclosure) males and females to be in departments having high scholastic emphasis (echoing Marcia and Friedman 1970), with females considering especially the employment opportunities associated with a particular department. Once in a department, that department's emphasis on social awareness appeared to facilitate identity stability and development for both men and women: in the absence of this emphasis, both sexes regressed in identity status. In Portugal, Costa and Campos (1986) found more high identity persons in the faculties of Law and Arts, and more Foreclosures in Engineering and Medicine. They attributed these differences to opportunities in the former faculties for discussion (and possible disequilibration) and the emphasis in the latter faculties on rote memory.

Examining differential effects of the college experience on the identity statuses, Waterman and Waterman (1970) reported that individuals who were Moratoriums in the occupational domain were the most dissatisfied with their college experience, and occupational Foreclosures were the most satisfied. In another study, Waterman and Waterman (1972) wrote that Moratoriums changed college major more frequently than did other statuses. Also, among college-leavers, Achievements did so for self-initiated reasons, but Foreclosures and Diffusions left in the face of negative external pressure (e.g., low grades). Rothman (1984) stated that Achievements and Foreclosures tended to be goal-oriented, but Diffusions got caught up in trivial obsessive-compulsive routines.

## Noncollege Youths

In two studies of identity development in noncollege settings, both Munro and Adams (1977) and Morash (1980) found more Achievements among working than among college youths. These investigators attributed this difference to the absence of an institutionalized psychosocial moratorium and the subsequent pressure to make life decisions. In a longitudinal study controlling for socioeconomic, age, and geographical effects, however, Archer and Waterman (1988) found that individuals attending college were more advanced in identity formation than those who were working or who were combining college attendance with work. These studies and those cited immediately above point to the need for describing contexts in terms of factors that facilitate or hinder psychosocial development.

## Adult Consequences of Initial Identity Formation
### Intimacy
An assumption in Erikson's theory is that successful resolution

of one psychosocial stage ought to affect directly the resolution of the next one. Hence, identity achievement should lead to successful resolution of the intimacy-isolation stage. All studies reviewed suggest that it does (Constantinople 1969; Craig-Bray et al. 1988; Hodgson and Fischer 1979; Kacerguis and Adams 1980; Kahn et al. 1985; Kinsler 1972; Schiedel and Marcia 1985; Tesch and Whitbourne 1982). Several of these researchers report that identity appears to precede intimacy for men, as Erikson assumed, but that identity and intimacy appear to codevelop in women. A more thorough review of intimacy research is in chapter 5 of Marcia et al. (1993).

## Longitudinal Studies after Late Adolescence

Marcia (1976) reported that 43 percent of Achievement and Moratorium males interviewed six to seven years later were still in these same statuses, whereas 84 percent of Foreclosures and Diffusions remained in the low identity statuses. Josselson (1987, 1988), in her informative account of the histories of women interviewed first in college and then fifteen years later, also saw a tendency for Diffusion to persist. Kroger, in a series of studies (1986, 1988, unpublished ms., and Kroger and Haslett 1987), has examined identity status transition pathways and change rates across interview domains.

## Identity Statuses in Adulthood

Both Amstey (1977) and Archer, Waterman, and Owens (1988) found that adult women who had returned to college to complete their education were more frequently Achievement or Moratorium than Foreclosure. Archer (1985b) and Owens et al. (1987) concluded that both identity and intimacy generally increased with age (see also Freilino and Hummel 1985) and early, *nonreflective* commitments tended to lead to subsequent disruptive life experiences among the statuses. (This finding may bode ill for the more numerous Foreclosure college marriages reported by Lutes [1981].) In addition, Identity Achievement women had liberated ideas about women's role and were high in masculinity; Moratorium women expressed some dissatisfaction with marriage; Foreclosures were traditional in attitudes toward women's role and high in femininity; and Diffusion women were high in masculinity and generally dissatisfied with marriage and parenting.

## Identity Development in Adulthood

Having formed an initial identity at late adolescence (Identity Achievement), an individual might be expected to undergo subsequent Moratorium Achievement (MAMA) cycles. As is clear in Marcia's (1976) follow-up study, however, not all adults do so. Some proceed through adulthood with their initial identity resolution unreconstructed and seem like Foreclosures. Studying identity development in adulthood, Whitbourne (1986) found that "openness to experience" predicted identity flexibility in adult men and women. Thinking along similar lines, Stephen et al. (1992) described two variables thought to predict to life-span identity development: dialectical reasoning and an experiential (as opposed to instrumental) outlook. Among university students, Moratoriums and Achievements tended to have a more experiential outlook and to be higher in dialecticism than Foreclosures and Diffusions. Significantly, Moratoriums were the highest of the statuses on both of these measures. Whether these variables will predict for adult development remains to be seen.

# Gender Differences in Identity Formation
## Content Areas of the Identity Status Interview

The foremost issue here is whether men and women differ in the relative importance of interview domains to their identity formation, and, specifically, whether interpersonal issues are more important to women's identity formation than to men's. That they are important to women has been established by Archer (1985a), Kroger (1983), Marcia and Friedman (1970), Schenkel and Marcia (1972), and Josselson (1988). That interpersonal concerns may be more important for women's identity than for men's is suggested by a fairly impressive number of studies (Archer 1989; Bilsker et al. 1988; Craig-Bray et al. 1988; Douvan and Adelson 1966; Hodgson and Fischer 1979; Josselson et al. 1977b; Kahn et al. 1985; Mellor 1989; Poppen 1974; Thorbecke and Grotevant 1982; C.K. Waterman and Nevid 1977). The foregoing does not mean, however, that interpersonal issues are not important for men's identity (Matteson 1977; Mellor 1989; Rogow et al. 1983). In his summary Mellor (1989) states: "[There may be] a connectedness theme in self-other development that is nonspecific to gender and that is useful for both males and females in generating relational self-definitions to resolve the identity crisis" (p. 372). Likewise, that interpersonal issues seem to have some predominance for women's identity formation does not mean that occupational and ideological issues are not important to them. Hopkins (1980, 1982), having constructed an "inner-space" interview to assess women's identity, had to conclude: "It is very clear from the present study that outer space concerns are no longer peripheral to female identity formation" (1982, 565). Confirming this result, Kroger (1986) found occupation to be the most highly ranked issue in importance for both male and female New Zealand university students, as did Bilsker et al. (1988) among a similar group in Canada. Although Archer (1989) found more Foreclosures among men than women (more women tending toward Achievement and Moratorium, especially in the family roles domain), she found few other gender differences in process, domain, or timing. Hence, Marcia's (1980) hypothesis that women's identity formation, because of its complexity, might take longer than men's was not supported. In fact, as Adams and Gulotta (1983) suggested and Streitmatter (1988) demonstrated, females may be chronologically ahead of males in the identity formation process. Following are, perhaps, the best summaries of this research to date. On women's identity development, Kroger (1983) states: "Rather than decisions about individual content areas, meta-decisions about how to balance competing identity contents and at the same time consider the implications for significant others seemed to capture identity concerns for many women from this sample" (p.15). Investigating gender differences in identity development in high school students. Thorbecke and Grotevant (1982) concluded ". . . it appears that for young men, vocational and interpersonal identity achievement proceed independently. . . . For young women, it appears important to negotiate identity achievement in the interpersonal domain in order to be engaged in occupational identity formation" (pp. 488–89).

## The Meaning of the Identity Statuses for Men and Women

Based upon many of the studies reviewed by Marcia (1980), it appeared that Foreclosure women were performing quite similarly to Identity Achievement women on a number of dependent variables. This finding led to the possibility that the Foreclosure status might have some adaptive significance for women that it did not have for men. From the perspective of ten more years of research, however, it appears that the earlier conclusions were erroneous. Out of eight studies with women conducted before 1977 in which a grouping of statuses could be ascertained, seven showed the Achievement-Foreclosure, Moratorium-Diffusion pattern. Since 1977, out of sixteen studies with discernible patterns, only four show the earlier grouping; the remaining twelve conform to theoretical expectations underlying the identity statuses. Of the two explanations for this change in pattern, the first is articulated by Orlofsky and Ginsburg (1981): "If Moratorium women are in fact developing beyond the conventional adjustment attained by Foreclosure women, we would expect them to excel on measures which go deeper than the surface level of functioning assessed by self-report and behavioral measures utilized in previous studies" (p. 299). When such "deeper," ego-structural measures are used, Moratorium women do perform positively, like Achievement women (Adams and Shea 1979; Ginsburg and Orlofsky 1981; Kroger 1988; Orlofsky and Frank 1986; Josselson 1982).

The second reason for changes in status ordering has to do with changes in social conditions: there has been a pattern of increasing support for women undergoing the choice and struggle involved in the identity development process (Morgan and Farber 1982). Identity research has not been isolated from the concerns of feminism. Stein and Weston (1982) found non-Traditional women to be more advanced in identity than Traditional women; and Prince-Embury and Deutchman (1981) reported that pro-ERA (Equal Rights Amendment) women scored higher on an identity measure than anti-ERA women. One variable in particular, fear of success, highlights the impact of social values on women's identity development. Studying college women, Howard (1975) found Identity Achievements' greater fear of success compared with the other statuses. In a definitive study on this variable, Orlofsky (1978), comparing college men and women, found that Identity Achievement and Moratorium women had higher achievement scores than did Foreclosures and Diffusions and also greater fear of success. He concluded:

> the high Fear of Success scores obtained by Achievement and especially Moratorium women are understandable as reflecting the conflicts which these more ambitious achieving women probably experience as they pursue ... less traditional more achievement-oriented goals. Since Foreclosure and Diffusion women are less motivated for academic vocational achievement, they experience less conflict between achievement strivings and traditional feminine role behaviors. ... (p. 60)

The effects of growing social support for women's achievement and identity formation is indicated in the post-1978 studies on fear of success by Freilino and Hummel (1985), who found Diffusion women to have the greatest fear of success, and Owens et al. (unpublished ms.), who found a negative relationship between identity achievement and fear of success.

In summary, whether because of more sophisticated measurement or for sociopolitical reasons or both, the issue of the grouping of the identity statuses for women is no longer problematical. Moratorium women resemble more closely Identity Achievement women than they do Foreclosure women. Also, even though the genders may arrive at identity via somewhat different pathways, the meaning of the identity statuses, as reflected in gender x status standings on dependent variables, seems similar. As Archer and Waterman (1988) conclude in an article on psychological individualism summarizing gender differences in sixteen identity studies: "Taken together, the results do not warrant concluding that gender differences exist with respect to this [identity] variable" (p. 69).

## Sex Roles and Identity

Although one's gender is a given with which one must come to

terms in constructing an identity, the degree to which one sub-
scribes to the roles and values socially assigned to one's gender
varies. Hence, one can be morphologically male, yet masculine,
feminine, androgynous, or undifferentiated in endorsement of
sex-role attitudes. The following group of studies take up the
differential effects of sex-role subscription on identity and intimacy development.

The first studies in this area were by Deldin (1977), who
found masculinity important for identity formation in college
males, and Orlofsky (1977), who reported masculinity and androgyny important for Identity Achievement in both college
men and women, and sex-role undifferentiated persons to be
Diffuse. Schiedel and Marcia (1985) replicated and extended
these findings. They report that masculinity was important for
identity development, especially for women, and that femininity was important to intimacy development, especially for men.
Androgynous persons tended to be high in both identity and intimacy. Studies using the identity statuses and other identity
measures and various sex-role inventories have replicated the
results above (Crown 1985; Della Selva and Dusek 1984; Fannin
1979; Grotevant and Thorbecke 1982; Tzuriel 1984; Waterman
and Whitbourne 1982). Except for Lamke and Peyton (1988),
who found only weak support in a study of high school students, across various measures of identity, intimacy, and sex-
role typing, the relationships among androgyny, high intimacy,
and high identity, as well as between masculinity and identity
and femininity and intimacy are fairly well established.

## Cross-Cultural Research

Two emphases are discernible in the cross-cultural studies reviewed. The first is the establishment of validity for the identity
statuses (and, by extension, Erikson's theoretical concept) in societies other than that of North America. Validity, here, does
not mean identical behavior. Foreclosures in a "foreclosed" setting ought not to be found behaving exactly like Foreclosures in
a setting that encourages moratoria. Rather, cross-cultural validity means that, taking into account the processes underlying an
identity status, one ought to be able to make verifiable predic-

tions about that status's behavior in a given cultural context. The second emphasis has been on extending our knowledge about identity development itself. Most of these studies are reviewed in the foregoing text. Table 7.1 lists studies involving other than Caucasian, North American populations. We recommend the original sources, for a review would be too lengthy for this chapter.

TABLE 7.1

CROSS-CULTURAL STUDIES ON IDENTITY

| Authors | Sample | Description |
|---|---|---|
| Matteson 1974 | Denmark | Family interaction |
| Chapman & Nicholls 1976 | New Zealand | Maori and Pakeha boys |
| Jegede 1976 | Nigeria | Comparative IAS[b] scores |
| Muto 1979 | Japan | Validation of ISI[c] |
| Kumar et al. 1980 | India | Managerial styles |
| Afrifah 1980 | Ghana | Formal operations |
| Arora 1981 | India | Marital dyads |
| Bosma, Graafsma 1982 et al.[a] | Holland | Development and GIDS[d] |
| Kato 1983 | Japan | Validation of ISI |
| Kroger 1983 et al. | New Zealand | ISI personality |
| Huh 1984 | South Korea | ISI domain importance |
| Owen 1984 | Cuban-American | ISI, IPD[e], self-esteem |
| Park 1994 | South Korea | Religiosity |
| Rall 1984 | South Africa | Identity-intimacy |
| Abraham 1986 | Mexican-American | Comparative patterns |
| Costa, Campos 1986 et al. | Portugal | Identity contexts |
| Streitmatter 1988 | Hispanic, Native American, Asian | Comparative |
| Phinney 1989 et al. | Black, Hispanic, Asian-American | Comparative |
| Rotheram-Boras 1989 | Black, Puerto Rican, Filipino | Comparative |
| Mohammed 1990 | Egypt | Validation of ISI |
| Mayeseless 1990 | Israel | Identity in army |
| Flum 1990 | Israel | High school identity |

a. Following a date, as here, "1982 et al." means that the same author(s) have produced similar works.
b. Identity Achievement Scale.
c. Identity Status Interview.
d. Groningen Identity Development Scale.
e. Inventory of Psycho-Social Development.

# References

Adams, G.R. 1985. Family correlates of female adolescents' ego-identity development. *Journal of Adolescence* 8:69–82.

Adams, G.R., Abraham, K.G., and Markstrom, C.A. 1987. The relations among identity development, self-consciousness, and self-focusing during middle and late adolescence. *Developmental Psychology* 23:292–97.

Adams, G.R., and Fitch, S.A. 1981. Ego stage and identity status development: A cross-lag analysis. *Journal of Adolescence* 4:163–71.

———. 1982. Ego stage and identity status development: A cross-sequential analysis. *Journal of Personality and Social Psychology* 43: 574–83.

———. 1983. Psychological environments at university departments: Effects on college students' identity status and ego stage development. *Journal of Personality and Social Psychology* 44:1266–75.

Adams, G.R., and Gulotta, T. 1983. *Adolescent life experiences*. Monterey, Calif.: Brooks/Cole.

Adams, G.R., Ryan, J.H., Hoffman, J.J., Dobson, W.R., and Nielsen, E.C. 1984. Ego identity status, conformity behavior, and personality in late adolescence. *Journal of Personality and Social Psychology* 47: 1091–1104.

Adams, G.R., and Shea, J.A. 1979. The relationship between identity status, focus of control, and ego development. *Journal of Youth and Adolescence* 8:81–89.

Afrifah, A. 1980. *The relationship between logical cognition and ego identity: An investigation of Piagetian and Eriksonian hypotheses about adolescence*. Doctoral dissertation, Columbia University, New York.

Amstey, F. 1977. *The relationship between continuing education and identity in adult women*. Doctoral dissertation, University of Rochester, N.Y.

Andrews, J. 1973. The relationship of values to identity achievement status. *Journal of Youth and Adolescence* 2:133–38.

Archer, S.L. 1982. The lower age boundaries of identity development. *Child Development* 53:1551–56.

———. 1985a. Career and family: The identity process for adolescent girls. *Youth and Society* 16:289–314.

———. 1985b. Identity and social roles. In A.S. Waterman (Ed.). *Identity in adolescence: Processes and contents*. New Directions for Child Development. Sourcebook #30. San Francisco: Jossey-Bass.

———. 1989. Gender differences in identity development: Issues of process, domain, and timing. *Journal of Adolescence* 12:117–38. Newbury Park, Calif.: Sage.

Archer, S.L., and Waterman, A.S. 1988. Psychological individualism: gender differences or gender neutrality? *Human Development* 31: 65–81.

Archer, S.L., Waterman, A.S., and Owens, P.O. 1988. Women's identity: Comparison among three patterns of life activities. Paper presented at the meeting of the Association for Women in Psychology, Bethesda, Md., March.

Bary, B. 1978. *Impact of parents in their adolescent son's identity crisis.* Doctoral dissertation, Temple University, Philadelphia.

Berzonsky, M.D. 1985. Diffusion within Marcia's identity status paradigm: Does it foreshadow academic problems? *Journal of Youth and Adolescence* 14:527–38.

———. 1989a. Identity style: Conceptualization and measurement. *Journal of Adolescent Research* 4:267–81.

———. 1989b. Self-theorists, identity status, and social cognition. In D.K. Lapsley and F.C. Power (Eds.). *Self, ego, and identity: Integrative approaches,* 243–62. New York: Springer-Verlag.

———. 1990. Self-construction over the life-span: A process perspective on identity formation. In G.J. Neimeyer and R.A. Neimeyer (Eds.). *Advances in personal construct theory,* 1:155–86. Greenwich, Conn.: JAI.

Berzonsky, M.D., and Barclay, C.T. 1981. Formal reasoning and identity formation: A reconceptualization. In J.A. Meacham and N.F. Santilli (Eds.). *Social development in youth: Structure and content.* Basel: Karger.

Berzonsky, M.D., and Niemeyer, G.J. 1988. Identity status and personal construct systems. *Journal of Adolescence* 11:195–204.

Berzonsky, M.D., Rice, K.G., and Neimeyer, G.J. 1990. Identity status and self-construct systems: Process x structure interactions. *Journal of Adolescence* 13:251–63.

Berzonsky, M.D., and Sullivan, C. 1992. Social-cognitive aspects of identity style: Need for cognition, experiential openness, and introspection. *Journal of Adolescent Research* 7:140–55.

Berzonsky, M.D., Weiner, A.S., and Raphael, D. 1975. Interdependence of formal reasoning. *Developmental Psychology* 11:258.

Bilsker, D., and Marcia, J.E. 1991. Adaptive regression and ego identity. *Journal of Adolescence* 14:75–84.

Bilsker, D., Schiedel, D., and Marcia, J. 1988. Sex differences in identity status. *Sex Roles* 18:231–36.

Blasi, A., and Hoeffel, J. 1974. Adolescence and formal operations. *Human Development* 17:344–63.

Blos, P. 1962. *On adolescence: A psychoanalytic interpretation.* New York: Free Press.

———. 1974. The genealogy of the ego ideal. *Psychoanalytic Study of the Child* 29:43–89.

Blustein, D.L., and Phillips, S.D. 1990. Relation between ego identity statuses and decision-making styles. *Journal of Counseling Psychology* 37:160–68.

Bob, S. 1968. *An investigation of the relationship between identity sta-*

*tus, cognitive style, and stress.* Doctoral dissertation, State University of New York at Buffalo, N.Y.

Bosma, H.A., and Gerrits, R.S. 1985. Family functioning and identity status in adolescence. *Journal of Early Adolescence* 5:69–80.

Bourne, E. 1978a. The state of research on ego identity: A review and appraisal. Part 1. *Journal of Youth and Adolescence* 7:223–51.

———. 1978b. The state of research on ego identity: A review and appraisal. Part 2. *Journal of Youth and Adolescence* 7:371–92.

Bowlby, J. 1969. *Attachment and loss: 1. Attachment.* New York: Basic Books.

Boyes, M.C., and Chandler, M. 1992. Cognitive development, epistemic doubt, and identity formation in adolescence. *Journal of Youth and Adolescence* 21, no. 3:277–304.

Bunt, M. 1968. Ego identity: Its relationship to the discrepancy between how an adolescent views himself and how he perceives that others view him. *Psychology* 5:14–25.

Caldwell, R.A., Bogat, G.A., and Cruise, K. 1989. The relationship of ego identity to social network structure and function in young men and women. *Journal of Adolescence* 12:309–13.

Campbell, E., Adams, G.R., and Dobson, W.R. 1984. Familial correlates of identity formation in late adolescence: A study of the predicted utility of connectedness and individuality in family relations. *Journal of Adolescence* 6:509–25.

Cauble, M.A. 1976. Formal operations, ego identity, and principled morality: Are they related? *Developmental Psychology* 12:362–64.

Cella, D.F., DeWolfe, A.S., and Fitzgibbon, M. 1987. Ego identity status, identification, and decision-making style in late adolescents. *Adolescence* 2:849–61.

Chandler, M. 1987. The Othello effect: An essay on the emergence and eclipse of skeptical doubt. *Human Development* 30:137–59.

Chapman, J.W., and Nicholls, J.G. 1976. Occupational identity status, occupational preference, and field dependence in Maori and Pakena boys. *Journal of Cross-Cultural Psychology* 7:61–72.

Constantinople, A. 1969. An Eriksonian measure of personality development in college students. *Developmental Psychology* 1:357–72.

Cooper, C.R., Grotevant, H.D., and Condin, S.M. 1983. Individuality and connectedness in the family as a context for adolescent identity formation and roletaking skill. In H.D. Grotevant and C.R. Cooper (Eds.). *Adolescent development in the family.* San Francisco: Jossey-Bass.

Costa, M.E., and Campos, B.P. 1986. Identity in university students: differences in course of study and gender. *Cadernos de Consulta Psicologica* 2:5–13.

———. 1988. A longitudinal study of identity development in university students. Paper presented at the First International Conference on Counseling Psychology and Human Development, Porto, Portugal,

July.

Côté, J.E., and Reker, G.T. 1979. Cognitive complexity and ego identity formation: A synthesis of cognitive and ego psychology. *Social Behavior and Personality* 7:107–12.

Craig-Bray, L., Adams, G.R., and Dobson, W.R. 1988. Identity formation and social relations during late adolescence. *Journal of Youth and Adolescence* 17:173–87.

Cross, H., and Allen, J. 1970. Ego identity status, adjustment, and academic achievement. *Journal of Consulting and Clinical Psychology* 34:288.

Crown, P.A. 1985. *Ego identity, intimacy, and sex role orientation of young adults.* Doctoral dissertation, University of Denver.

Deldin, L.S. 1977. *Sex role development and identity achievement.* Doctoral dissertation, University of Florida, Gainesville.

Della Selva, P.D., and Dusek, J.B. 1984. Sex role orientation and resolution of Eriksonian crises during the late adolescent years. *Journal of Personality and Social Psychology* 47:204–12.

Dellas, M., and Jernigan, L.P. 1987. Occupational identity status development, gender comparisons, and internal-external control in first-year Air Force cadets. *Journal of Youth and Adolescence* 16: 587–600.

Donovan, J.M. 1970. *A study of ego identity formation.* Doctoral dissertation, University of Michigan, Ann Arbor.

———. 1975. Identity status and interpersonal style. *Journal of Youth and Adolescence* 4:37–55.

Douvan, E., and Adelson, J. 1966. *The adolescent experience.* New York: Wiley.

Dufresne, J., and Cross, J.H. 1972. *Personality variables in student drug use.* Master's thesis, University of Connecticut, Storrs.

Enright, R.D., Lapsley, D.U., Drivas, A.E., and Fehr, L.A. 1980. Parental influences on the development of adolescent autonomy and identity. *Journal of Youth and Adolescence* 9:526–45.

Erikson, E.H. 1952. *Healthy personality development in children: As related to programs of the federal government.* (Remarks made at an interagency conference at Princeton, N.J.) New York: Josiah Macy Jr. Foundation.

———. 1987. Remarks on the "wider identity." In S. Schlein (Ed.). *A way of looking at things.* New York: Norton.

Fannin, P.N. 1979. The relation between ego identity status and sex role attitude, work role salience, atypicality of major, and self-esteem in college women. *Journal of Vocational Behavior* 14:12–22.

Freilino, M.K., and Hummel, R. 1985. Achievement and identity in college age vs. adult women students. *Journal of Youth and Adolescence* 14:1–11.

Genthner, R.W., and Neuber, K.A. 1975. Identity achievers and their rated levels of facilitation. *Psychological Reports* 36:754.

Gilligan, C. 1982. *In a different voice: Psychological theory and women's development.* Cambridge: Harvard University Press.

Ginsburg, S.D., and Orlofsky, J.L. 1981. Ego identity status, ego development, and locus of control in college women. *Journal of Youth and Adolescence* 10:297–307.

Goldman, J.A., Rosenzweig, M., and Lutter, A.D. 1980. Effect of ego identity statuses on interpersonal attraction. *Journal of Youth and Adolescence* 9:153–62.

Gombosi, P.G. 1972. *Regression in the service of the ego as a function of identity status.* Doctoral dissertation, Boston University.

Grossman, S.M., Shea, J.A., and Adams, G.R. 1980. Effects of parental divorce during early childhood on ego development and identity formation of college students. *Journal of Divorce* 3:263–72.

Grotevant, H.D., and Cooper, C.R. 1983. The role of family communication patterns in adolescent identity and role-taking. Paper presented at the meeting of the Society for Research in Child Development, Detroit.

———. 1985. Patterns of interaction in family relationships and the development of identity exploration in adolescence. *Child Development* 56:415–28.

———. 1986. Individuation in family relationships: A perspective on individual differences in the development of identity and roletaking skill in adolescence. *Human Development* 29:82–100.

Grotevant, H.D., and Thorbecke, W.L. 1982. Sex differences in styles of occupational identity formation in late adolescence. *Developmental Psychology* 18:396–405.

Hauser, S.T. 1976. Loevinger's model of ego development: A critical review. *Psychological Bulletin* 83:928–57.

Hodgson, J.W., and Fischer, J.L. 1979. Sex differences in identity and intimacy development in college youth. *Journal of Youth and Adolescence* 8:37–50.

Hogan, R. 1973. Moral conduct and moral character: A psychological perspective. *Psychological Bulletin* 79:217–32.

Hopkins, L.B. 1980. Inner space and outerspace identity in contemporary females. *Psychiatry* 43:1–12.

———. 1982. Assessment of identity status in college women using outer space and innerspace interviews. *Sex Roles* 8:557–66.

Howard, M.R. 1975. *Ego identity status in women, fear of success, and performance in a competitive situation.* Doctoral dissertation, State University of New York at Buffalo, N.Y.

Hult, R.E. 1979. The relationship between ego identity status and moral reasoning in university women. *Journal of Psychology* 103:203–7.

Hummel, R., and Roselli, L.L. 1983. Identity status and academic achievement in female adolescents. *Adolescence* 17:17–27.

Jones, R.M., and Hartmann, B.R. 1988. Ego identity: Developmental differences and experimental substance use among adolescents. *Jour-*

*nal of Adolescence* 11:347–60.

Jones, R.M., and Streitmatter, J.L. 1987. Validity and reliability of the EOM-EIS for early adolescents. *Adolescence* 22:647–59.

Jordan, D. 1970. *Parental antecedents of ego identity formation.* Master's thesis. State University of New York at Buffalo, N.Y.

Josselson, R.L. 1972. *Identity formation in college women.* Doctoral dissertation, University of Michigan, Ann Arbor.

———. 1973. Psychodynamic aspects of identity formation in college women. *Journal of Youth and Adolescence* 2:3–51.

———. 1980. Ego development in adolescence. In J. Adelson (Ed.). *Handbook of adolescent psychology.* New York: Wiley.

———. 1982. Personality structure and identity status in women viewed through early memories. *Journal of Youth and Adolescence* 11: 293–99.

———. 1987. Identity diffusion: A long-term follow-up. *Adolescent Psychiatry.* Vol. XIV. Chicago: University of Chicago Press.

———. 1988. *Finding herself: pathways of identity development in women.* New York: Jossey-Bass.

Josselson, R.L., Greenberger, E., and McConochie, D. 1977a. Phenomenological aspects of psychosocial maturity in adolescence. Part 1. Boys. *Journal of Youth and Adolescence* 6:25–55.

———. 1977b. Phenomenological aspects of psychosocial maturity in adolescence. Part 2. Girls. *Journal of Youth and Adolescence* 6: 145–67.

Kacerguis, M.A., and Adams, G.R. 1980. Erikson stage resolution: The relationship between identity and intimacy in midlife. *Journal of Youth and Adolescence* 9:117–26.

Kahn, R.L., Zimmerman, G., and Getzels, J.W. 1985. Relationships between identity in young adulthood and intimacy in midlife. *Journal of Personality and Social Psychology* 49:1316–22.

Kamptner, N.L. 1988. Identity development in late adolescence: Causal modeling of social and familial influences. *Journal of Youth and Adolescence* 17:493–514.

Kelly, G. 1955. *The psychology of personal constructs.* 2 vols. New York: Norton.

Kendis, R.J., and Tan, A.L. 1978. Ego identity perception of parents among female college students. *Perceptual and Motor Skills* 47:1201–2.

Kinsler, P. 1972. *Ego identity status and intimacy.* Doctoral dissertation, State University of New York at Buffalo, N.Y.

Kirby, C.S. 1977. *Complexity-simplicity as a dimension of identity formation.* Doctoral dissertation, Michigan State University, East Lansing.

Kohlberg, L. 1976. Moral stages and moralization: The cognitive developmental approach. In T. Lickona (Ed.). *Moral development and moral behavior.* New York: Holt, Rinehart and Winston.

Kohlberg, L., and Gilligan, C. 1972. The adolescent as a philosopher: The discovery of the self in a post–conventional world. In J. Kagan and R. Coles (Eds.) *12 to 16: Early adolescence,* 144–80. New York: Norton.

Kohut, H. 1971. *The analysis of the self: A systematic approach to the treatment of narcissistic personality disorders.* New York: International University Press.

Kroger, J. 1983. A developmental study of identity formation among late adolescent and adult women. *Psychological Documents* 13 (ms. no. 2537).

———. 1985. Separation-individuation and ego identity status in New Zealand university students. *Journal of Youth and Adolescence* 14:133–47.

———. 1986. The relative importance of identity status interview components: Replication and extension. *Journal of Adolescence* 9:337–54.

———. 1988. A longitudinal study of ego identity status interview domains. *Journal of Adolescence* 11:49–64.

———. 1990. Ego structuralization in adolescence as seen through early memories and ego identity status. *Journal of Adolescence* 13: 65–77.

Kroger, J., and Haslett, S.J. 1987. A retrospective study of ego identity status change by mid-life adults. *Social and Behavioral Sciences Documents* 17 (ms. no. 2797).

Kurfiss, J. 1981. *Cognitive development: Sine qua non of identity achievement?* Paper presented at the meeting of the Rocky Mountain Psychological Association, Denver.

Lamke, L.K., and Peyton, K.G. 1988. Adolescent sex-role orientation and ego identity. *Journal of Adolescence* 11:205–15.

LaVoie, J.C. 1976. Ego identity formation in middle adolescence. *Journal of Youth and Adolescence* 5:371–85.

Leadbetter, B.J., and Dionne, J.P. 1981. The adolescent's use of formal operational thinking in solving problems related to identity resolution. *Adolescence* 16:111–21.

Leiper, R.N. 1981. *The relationship of cognitive developmental structures to the formation of identity in young men.* Doctoral dissertation, Simon Fraser University, Burnaby, British Columbia.

Loevinger, J., and Wessler, R. 1970. *Measuring ego development.* 2 vols. San Francisco: Jossey-Bass.

Lutes, C. 1981. Early marriage and identity foreclosure. *Adolescence* 16:809–16.

Mahler, M.S., Pine, F., and Bergman, A. 1975. *The psychological birth of the human infant.* New York: Basic Books.

Marcia, J.E. 1966. Development and validation of ego identity status. *Journal of Personality and Social Psychology* 3:551–58.

———. 1967. Ego identity status: Relationship to change in self-esteem, "general maladjustment," and authoritarianism. *Journal of Person-*

*ality* 35:119–33.

———. 1976. Identity six years after: a follow-up study. *Journal of Youth and Adolescence* 5:145–60.

———. 1980. Identity in adolescence. In J. Adelson (Ed.). *Handbook of adolescent psychology.* New York: Wiley.

———. 1983. Some directions for the investigation of ego identity development in early adolescence. *Journal of Early Adolescence* 3: 215–23.

Marcia, J.E., and Friedman, M. 1970. Ego identity status in college women. *Journal of Personality* 38:249–62.

Marcia, J.E., Waterman, A.S., Matteson, D.R., Archer, S.L., and Orlofsky, J.L. (Eds.). 1993. *Ego Identity: A Handbook for Research.* New York: Springer-Verlag.

Matteson, D.R. 1974. *Alienation vs. exploration and commitment: Personality and family correlates of adolescent identity statuses.* Report for the Project for Youth Research. Copenhagen Royal Danish School of Educational Studies, Denmark.

———. 1975. *Adolescence today: Sex roles and the search for destiny.* Homewood, Ill.: Dorsey.

———. 1977. Exploration and commitment: Sex differences: methodological problems in the use of the identity status categories. *Journal of Youth and Adolescence* 6:353–79.

Meilman, P.W. 1979. Cross-section age changes in ego identity status during adolescence. *Developmental Psychology* 15:230–31.

Mellor, S. 1989. Gender differences in identity formation as a function of self-other relationships. *Journal of Youth and Adolescence* 18: 361–75.

Morash, M.A. 1980. Working class membership and the adolescent identity crisis. *Adolescence* 15:313–20.

Morgan, E., and Farber, B.A. 1982. Toward a reformulation of the Eriksonian model of female identity development. *Adolescence* 17: 199–211.

Munro, G., and Adams, G.R. 1977. Ego identity formation in college students and working youth. *Developmental Psychology* 13:523–24.

Neimeyer, G.J., and Rareshide, M.B. 1991. Personal memories and personal identity: The impact of ego identity development on autobiographical memory recall. *Journal of Personality and Social Psychology* 60:562–69.

Neuber, K.A., and Genthner, R.W. 1977. The relationship between ego identity, personal responsibility, and facilitative communication. *Journal of Psychology* 95:45–49.

Newman, F. 1986. *Ego development in women in an urban hostel.* Doctoral dissertation, Simon Fraser University, Burnaby, British Columbia.

Orlofsky, J.L. 1977. Sex role orientation, identity formation, and self-esteem in college men and women. *Sex Roles* 3:561–74.

———. 1978. The relationship between intimacy status and antecedent personality components. *Adolescence* 8:419–41.

Orlofsky, J.L., and Frank, M. 1986. Personality structure as viewed through early memories and identity status in college men and women. *Journal of Personality and Social Psychology* 50:580–86.

Orlofsky, J.L., and Ginsburg, S.D. 1981. Intimacy status: Relationship to affect cognition. *Adolescence* 16:91–100.

Orlofsky, J.L., Marcia, J.E., and Lesser, I.M. 1973. Ego identity status and the intimacy versus isolation crisis of young adulthood. *Journal of Personality and Social Psychology* 27:211–19.

Oshman, H.P., and Manosevitz, M. 1974. The impact of the identity crisis on the adjustment of late adolescent males. *Journal of Youth and Adolescence* 3:207–16.

Owens, P.A., Archer, S.L., and Waterman, A.S. 1987. *Women's identity and work orientation: Comparisons among four life styles.* Manuscript. Trenton State College, N.J.

Pack, A.T., Brill, N.Q., and Christie, R.L. 1976. Quitting marijuana. *Diseases of the Nervous System,* 37:205–9.

Papini, D.R., Sebby, R.A., and Clark, S. 1989. Affective quality of family relations and adolescent identity exploration. *Adolescence* 26: 457–66.

Piaget, J. 1965. *The moral judgement of the child.* M. Gabain (Trans.). New York: Free Press.

Podd, M.H. 1972. Ego identity status and morality: The relationship between two developmental constructs. *Developmental Psychology* 6:497–507.

Podd, M.H., Marcia, J.E., and Rubin, B.M. 1970. The effects of ego identity and partner perception on a prisoner's dilemma game. *Journal of Social Psychology* 82:117–26.

Poppen, P.J. 1974. *The development of sex differences in moral judgment for college males and females.* Doctoral dissertation, Cornell University, Ithaca, N.Y.

Prager, K.J. 1982. Identity development and self-esteem in young women. *Journal of Genetic Psychology* 141:177–82.

Prince-Embury, S., and Deutchman, I.E. 1981. The identity status of politically active pro- and anti-ERA women. *Journal of Mind and Behavior* 2:309–21.

Raphael, D. 1975. *An investigation into aspects of identity status of high school females.* Doctoral dissertation, University of Toronto.

———. 1977. Identity status in university women: A methodological note. *Journal of Youth and Adolescence* 6:57–62.

Rasmussen, J.E. 1964. Relationship of ego identity to psychosocial effectiveness. *Psychological Reports* 15:815–25.

Read, D., Adams, G.R., and Dobson, W.R. 1984. Ego identity status, personality and social influence style. *Journal of Personality and Social Psychology* 46:169–77.

Rogow, A.M., Marcia, J.E., and Slugoski, B.R. 1983. The relative importance of identity status interview components. *Journal of Youth
and Adolescence* 9:87–99.

Rothman, K.M. 1984. Multivariate analysis of the relationship of personal concerns to adolescent ego identity status. *Adolescence* 19:
713–27.

Rotter, J.B. 1966. Generalized expectancies for internal versus external
control of reinforcement. *Psychological Monographs* 80 (1): Whole
no. 609.

Rowe, I., and Marcia, J.E. 1980. Ego identity status, formal operations,
and moral development. *Journal of Youth and Adolescence* 9:
87–99.

St. Clair, S., and Day, H.P. 1979. Ego identity status and values among
young females. *Journal of Youth and Adolescence* 8:317–26.

Schenkel, S. 1975. Relationship among ego identity status, field-indepen-
dence, and traditional femininity. *Journal of Youth and Adolescence* 4:73–82.

Schenkel, S., and Marcia, J.E. 1972. Attitudes toward premarital inter-
course in determining ego identity status in college women. *Journal of Personality* 3:472–82.

Schiedel, D.G., and Marcia, J.E. 1985. Ego identity, intimacy, sex role orientation, and gender. *Developmental Psychology* 18:149–60.

Shain, L., and Farber, B.K. 1989. Female identity development and self-
reflection in late adolescence. *Adolescence* 24:381–92.

Skoe, E.E., and Marcia, J.E. 1991. The development and partial validation
of a care-based measure of moral development. *Merrill-Palmer
Quarterly* 37:289–304.

Slugoski, B.R., Marcia, J.E., and Koopman, R.F. 1984. Cognitive and social interactional characteristics of ego identity statuses in college
males. *Journal of Personality and Social Psychology* 47:646–61.

Stein, S.L., and Weston, L.C. 1982. Collge women's attitudes toward
women and identity achievement. *Adolescence* 17:895–99.

Stephen, J., Fraser, E., and Marcia, J.E. 1992. Moratorium-achievement
(MAMA) cycles in lifespan identity development: Value orienta-
tions and reasoning system. *Journal of Adolescence* 15:283–300.

Sterling, C.M., and Van Horn, K.R. 1989. Identity and death anxiety. *Adolescence* 24:321–26.

Streitmatter, J.L. 1988. Ethnicity as a mediating variable of early adolescent identity development. *Journal of Adolescence* 11:335–46.

———. 1989. Identity development and academic achievement in early
adolescence. *Journal of Early Adolescence* 9:99–116.

Streitmatter, J.L., and Pate, G. 1989. Identity status development and
cognitive prejudice in early adolescents. *Journal of Early Adolescence* 9:142–52.

Sullivan, H.S. 1953. *The interpersonal theory of psychiatry*. New York:
Norton.

Tesch, S.A., and Cameron, K.A. 1987. Openness to experience and development of adult identity. *Journal of Personality* 55:615–30.

Tesch, S.A., and Whitbourne, S.K. 1982. Intimacy and identity status in young adults. *Journal of Personality and Social Psychology* 43: 1041–51.

Thorbecke, W., and Grotevant, H.D. 1982. Gender differences in interpersonal identity formation. *Journal of Youth and Adolescence* 11:479–92.

Toder, N.L., and Marcia, J.E. 1973. Ego identity status and response to conformity pressure in college women. *Journal of Personality and Social Psychology* 26:287–94.

Tzuriel, D. 1984. Sex role typing and ego identity in Israeli, Oriental, and Western adolescents. *Journal of Personality and Social Psychology* 46:440–57.

Tzuriel, D., and Klein, M.M. 1977. Ego identity: Effects of ethnocentrism, ethnic identification, and cognitive complexity in Israeli, Oriental, and Western ethnic groups. *Psychological Reports* 40: 1099–1110.

Wagner, J.A. 1987. Formal operations and ego identity in adolescence. *Adolescence* 22:23–35.

Waterman, A.S. 1982. Identity development from adolescence to adulthood: An extension of theory and a review of research. *Developmental Psychology* 18:342–58.

Waterman, A.S., and Archer, S.L. 1979. Ego identity status and expressive writing among high school and college students. *Journal of Youth and Adolescence* 8:327–41.

Waterman, A.S., Geary, P.S., and Waterman, C.K. 1974. Longitudinal study of changes in ego identity status from the freshman to the senior year at college. *Developmental Psychology* 10:387–92.

Waterman, A.S., and Goldman, J.A. 1976. A longitudinal study of ego identity development at a liberal arts college. *Journal of Youth and Adolescence* 5:361–69.

Waterman, A.S., Kohutis, E., and Pulone, J. 1977. The role of expressive writing in identity formation. *Developmental Psychology* 13:286–87.

Waterman, A.S., and Waterman, C.K. 1970. The relationship between ego identity status and satisfaction with college. *Journal of Educational Research* 64:165–68.

———. 1972. Relationship between freshman identity status and subsequent academic behavior: A test of the predictive validity of Marcia's categorization system for identity status. *Developmental Psychology* 6:179.

Waterman, A.S., and Whitbourne, S.K. 1982. Androgyny and psychosocial development among college students and adults. *Journal of Personality* 50:121–33.

Waterman, C.K., Beubel, M., and Waterman, A.S. 1970. Relationship between resolution of the identity crisis and outcomes of previous psychosocial crises. Proceedings of the 78th Annual Convention of the American Psychological Association, 467–68.

Waterman, C.K., and Nevid, J.S. 1977. Sex differences in the resolution of the identity crisis. *Journal of Youth and Adolescence* 6:337–42.

Waterman, C.K., and Waterman, A.S. 1974. Ego identity status and decision styles. *Journal of Youth and Adolescence* 3:1–6.

———. 1975. Fathers and sons: A study of ego identity across two generations. *Journal of Youth and Adolescence* 4:331–38.

Werner, H. 1957. The concept of development from a comparative and organismic point of view. In D.B. Harris (Ed.). *The concept of development*, 125–48. Minneapolis: University of Minnesota Press.

Whitbourne, S.K. 1986. Openness to experience, identity flexibility, and life changes in adults. *Journal of Personality and Social Psychology* 50:163–68.

# 8

# Renegotiating Chinese Identity: Between Local Group and National Ideology

## by Kristen Parris

Is it "fast, lively, new, convenient, and rich," or is it nothing more than "smuggling, grave sites, pornography, fakery, and swindling"?[1] This is the question many were asking during the 1980s when the debate over the "Wenzhou model" of development raged in the People's Republic of China. With its expansive private household–based industry and trade, Wenzhou's economy attracted national attention throughout the decade. At the center of the debate was this question: "Is Wenzhou capitalism or is it socialism (*xing zi xing she*)?"

This debate was ostensibly about the direction of economic development in one prefecture situated on the southeastern corner of Zhejiang Province, facing the East China Sea and Taiwan. But the Wenzhou debate was ultimately not just about Wenzhou or even correct economic development strategies. It was most fundamentally about national identity, who defines it,

---

*Note:* The analytic uses of the theory of identity developed in previous chapters are illustrated in this account of political change in China. The author, a China specialist, interviewed workers, merchants, and political officials in Wenzhou, on the East China Sea, to see how the dynamics of change were being affected by struggles over group identity. As we see, the emergence of a new regional identity opens the door to more pervasive changes in Chinese society.

and what forms of political and social behavior become justified as a consequence.

The renegotiation of a local Wenzhou identity was one part of the struggle to define a national identity in the People's Republic of China. With the reforms that began in the late 1970s, the voices and practices of ethnic minorities, youth, clans, and local communities emerged and called into question centrally defined standards for behavior, lifestyle, success, morality, and common sense. In doing so they opened up a new conversation about what it means to be Chinese and a new struggle over who should decide.

Identity has been used in a variety of ways by social scientists.[2] At its most fundamental, identity concerns, as Perry Link suggests, "a sense of being the same with something larger, those larger things being (a) ideologies and (b) various groups." It is, as Link proposes, the obverse of a more familiar Marxist category, "alienation," meaning separation from self and society.[3]

The case of Wenzhou illuminates the nature of group identifications and the sense in which they supplant the commitments of a faltering ideology. In this case, the group aspect of identification was the basis for the subversion of its ideological aspect. Indeed, in the more specific formulation offered by Crawford Young, the case allows us to explore the various aspects of identity: as "primordial attachment based in real or imagined family or blood ties; as the basis for instrumental collective action; and as a social construction and symbolic category that is invented or imagined through a variety or interactions and is subject to on-going negotiation.[4] In Wenzhou, local or native place ties grew out of particular geographic, linguistic, and historical conditions and were reinforced after 1949 by central state policies. They became the basis for community solidarity in the face of a hostile central state, and a symbol, both negative and positive, that ultimately developed into a challenge to the official socialist proletarian nationalism of the CCP.

When localism raises questions about the national identity, whether as a separatist movement or as doubt about national self-definition,[5] it necessarily tests central definitions of national identity and, therefore, state authority and power. National identity is always linked to the political hegemony and legitimacy of the state. As Ernest Gellner argues, nationalism is a theory of political legitimacy that determines the norm for the legitimacy of political units in the modern world.[6] Local ties do not, however, necessarily portend the ultimate disintegration of the nation. They may instead offer alternative bases for the reintegration of society and a new national identity. In this struggle between central and local identity a contest can be seen between hegemony and the assertion of an alternative with far-reaching consequences for the future of China.

# Center and Locality in China
## Local Ties in Traditional China

Local ties have always been important in China. The geographical and cultural differences between China's different regions are stark and often became the basis for rivalries, jealousies, and factionalism. It was traditionally accepted by the Chinese state that each locality had its own customs. Indeed, one dimension of being Chinese was to have a native place origin from somewhere in China. These ties were important to people when they left home for family, religious, commercial, or governmental reasons. Native place ties were the basis for the organization of merchant guilds (*hui-guan*) and native place associations (*tong-xianghui*) around the empire and were of great significance in shaping the development of urban economies. Some scholars have suggested that the institutionalization of local solidarities produced more open and yet integrated civic order.[7] As we have seen in chapter 5 of this book, the basis for the tolerance of differences essential to a national identity rests with an assurance of one's own particular group identity. A strong identity consists of an appropriate tension between the indigenous and the universal.

In monarchical China, local elites, who conformed to the standards of and were accepted by the center, were expected to glorify their place of origin and their local traits and customs.[8] The key to order was harmonizing multiple identifications, family, kinship group, native place, country. James Watson argues that, traditionally, to be Chinese was to conform to a set of standardized rites and symbols prescribed by the center. The boundaries between Chinese and non-Chinese was fluid as "barbarian" groups came to accept these rites and symbols.[9]

A Confucian approach to moral knowledge and appropriate behavior was institutionalized in the examination system and a centralized bureaucracy. There was, however, a relatively low degree of bureaucratic penetration into local society that left space for considerable autonomy and variation. Although failure to enforce the state's orthodoxy and control local communities was seen as leading to chaos, a high degree of variation was expected within an overarching unity. Combined with the unified ideographic writing system and a hierarchy of marketing structures and commercial centers, the result was a high degree of cultural integration and a strong sense of cultural Chinese identity that lasted until the early twentieth century, when the last dynasty collapsed and a unified China gave way to fragmentation and disintegration.[10]

## Localism in the PRC

The Chinese Communist Party (CCP) came to power looking to use ideology as the means of uniting China into a modern nation-state. The official Marxism-Leninism of the CCP asserts the existence of a common national identity centered on the interest represented by the party. Thus, individuals are understood to be among "the people" when they share an interest in national unity, prosperity, and the development of socialism, as defined by the CCP. Otherwise they are the enemies of the people, of socialism, and of China. In this formulation, to be Chinese is to be loyal and grateful to the party-state and its Marxist-Leninist orthodoxy and to oppose imperialism, feudalism, and capitalism. The CCP, like Leninist parties in power elsewhere, set out to negate the old society as weak and feudal, to purge the nation of foreign influence, and to proletarianize Chinese society. Leninism and Maoism required that all societal interests and identities were to be defined by and subordinate to the party, leaving little room for the authentic cultural pluralism of local groupings. Moreover, the new communist state not only had greater ambitions for imposing central orthodoxy on local society, it had greater capacity to do so.

Although there is some debate about the extent to which

the center actually penetrated and controlled rural villages, the CCP always insisted that local concerns must give way to party-defined national interests and ideals.[11] Moreover, there was much about local practices in China to offend the official orthodoxy. Religious rituals and rites flew in the face of state atheism, while local strategies for economic survival and success often violated central definitions of socialism. The central party-state attempted to enforce local responsiveness to central commands through its system of appointments, the *nomenklatura* system.[12] The party's Central Committee controlled appointments, promotion, and removal of government and party officials at all levels.

Localism did not entirely disappear, however, as local cadres strained to ensure the economic viability, if not always the prosperity, of their own regions. Over time, the central-local relationship developed from a highly centralized and coercive command relationship to one that is more decentralized and based on negotiation.[13] One local strategy was to gain the status of a model of development worthy of praise and emulation. The most famous of local models is Dazhai, which became an example of peasant virtue and self-reliance in the 1960s, catapulting its leaders to national power.[14] In the 1980s Wenzhou was promoted by some as a model of economic development. While Dazhai was a model of antimarket collectivism cultivated by the state, the Wenzhou model grew out of a resistance to the central orthodoxy and was based on the local economic culture characterized by extensive commodification and peasant entrepreneurialism.

# The Roots of Group Identity in Wenzhou

Wenzhou's strong localism is rooted in shared history, language, economic practices, and popular rituals that distinguish the region not only from Mandarin-speaking northerners (who live north of the Yangzi River) but also from those who live in the northern part of Zhejiang Province.[15] Wenzhou's special geographic and language traits have been reinforced since 1949 by a shared historical experience and by central policy.

## Geography

Shielded by the mountainous hinterland and islands scattered along the coast, Wenzhou has historically been notorious for piracy, banditry, smuggling, and general lawlessness.[16] The prefecture incorporates and administers nine counties and two urban districts. With a population of nearly 7 million, most of the population are labeled Han, the dominant ethnic group in the PRC;[17] it is the most populous and most densely populated of Zhejiang's prefectures.[18] While the plains of northern Zhejiang have been known as the land of rice and fish (*mi yu shi zhou*), mountainous terrain and resource shortages made life in Wenzhou's region more difficult. The dense population and scarcity of land made handicrafts and household-based petty trading and production necessary to supplement agriculture, leading to the early development of a commodity economy in the region. Overpopulation forced many to migrate either to other parts of China as cotton teasers and itinerant traders of local goods or beyond China as part of a large overseas community. Such economic practices, especially petty commodity production and commerce, have become associated with Wenzhou and are emblematic of the local identity.

Far-flung Wenzhounese travelers are themselves significant for Wenzhou's local identity. In efforts to describe what was different about Wenzhou, people would often point to the long distances Wenzhounese traveled to do business. If there is business to be done, a Wenzhounese will be there to do it—in Tibet, Inner Mongolia, and the Sino-Russian border. Away from home, Wenzhounese maintain ties, joining together to do business and live on "Wenzhou streets" all over the country and beyond. Today Wenzhou claims over 100,000 Wenzhou natives living abroad in forty-seven countries.[19] Most are in Southeast Asia, but there is a large Wenzhou population in Paris and a growing community in New York. Ties among Wenzhou people abroad are maintained outside China through the *tongxiang hui*. These associations, such as the one in New York City, provide mutual support and contacts and act as bridges between Wenzhou and the world.[20]

Thus, although Wenzhou was isolated from the hinterland by rough terrain, its location on the coast allowed for greater contact with the outside world than was true of many inland regions. Wenzhou became a major trading port beginning in the Southern Sung Dynasty (1127–1278). In 1876, Wenzhou became one of the treaty ports forcibly opened up by the treaty of Chefoo, with extraterritoriality and its customs duties under British control. While Wenzhou never gained the status of the larger ports such as Shanghai, Canton, or Tianjin, and even in Zhejiang was overshadowed by Ningbo to the north, the early foreign presence in Wenzhou, together with the overseas community, raised awareness of alternative ways of life. Consciousness of alternative ways of life is often part of identity formation in a region as remote from the center of national power and culture as Wenzhou.[21]

## Language

Southerners in China are distinguished from northerners by their non-Mandarin dialects (or languages).[22] Wenzhou was further isolated from the rest of Zhejiang Province by its distinct local speech. A 1955 report stated that the Wenzhou dialect was understood only by those living within a radius of thirty-four miles of the city radio station and that only 5 percent of the people in Wenzhou could understand Mandarin, the official language of the national capital in the north.[23] The distinctiveness of the local language is a source of both amusement and pride. Several people claimed in conversations with me that their language is so unusual that it was used as a secret code for communication during the war with Vietnam in the late 1970s.[24] This linguistic distinctiveness, when coupled with local cultural practices, suggests a kind of regional, even quasi-ethnic identity. Perhaps because of the relative wealth of the region, this distinctiveness never gave rise to the prejudice or discrimination that has sometimes plagued other distinctive local groups when they have traveled outside their home regions.[25]

## Communist Policy

During the Anti-Japanese war and the civil war with the Nationalists in the 1930s and 1940s, local communist guerrilla forces were strong in Wenzhou, and the region was peacefully "self-liberated" by local forces in 1949. Cut off from the sup-

THE POWER OF IDENTITY

port, direction, and control of the party center, guerrilla forces in Wenzhou adapted to local conditions, undertook an economic policy of promoting the local commodity economy, and thereby developed an alliance with local landlords and business circles.[26]

After 1949, the historic path of local practices combined with antimarket central policy to create tension with the national center and reinforce local solidarities further. Wenzhou was considered a strategically vulnerable front line (qianxian) against Nationalist forces in Taiwan. Because the Mao government would not develop vulnerable areas, Wenzhou received little in the way of central investment. This meant that few jobs depended on nationally funded state-owned enterprise. For most of the period when there was minimal state investment, party policy criminalized private economic activity.[27] These economic, cultural, and political constraints forced the population to rely on local resources and played a critical role in the expansion of underground, unofficial, or private economic activities that were often illegal and almost always counter to national values and lent to Wenzhou's people a negative identity in the era of Mao's socialism.

## Wenzhou as a Negative Identity
### Labeling as State Policy

One function of group identity is to idealize one way of life at the expense of others. In the same manner as dominant groups marginalize particular ethnic, racial, or gender groups by ascribing negative traits to them, so do regimes generally try to weaken competing loyalties by denigration and labeling.[28]

As the CCP attempted to consolidate its power and define a national identity for China that would underpin the authority and power of the party, it assigned negative labels to those groups representing alternative interpretations of what it meant to be Chinese. The CCP represented itself as the savior of the Chinese nation both from foreign imperialists and from the weak and feudal Chinese past. Thus, intellectuals were repeatedly attacked as untrustworthy bearers of feudal cultural values and supporters of Western bourgeois liberalization. Those engaged in capitalist pursuits were portrayed not only as exploiters but as tainted by foreign attachments or sentiments. Even small-scale private entrepreneurialism was denigrated as money- grubbing profiteering and speculation—the "tails of capitalism."

The use of official labels—good (proletarians, cadres, revolutionary) and bad (rightist, capitalist, bourgeois)—became an institutionalized practice that created new collective group consciousness.[29] These labels typically identified individuals and located them in groups with others so identified. They could be applied to entire localities as well. The Maoist model of Dazhai was a model of proletarian socialist values. Wenzhou, in contrast, became a negative model—a model of "capitalist restoration."

## The Capitalist Restoration in Wenzhou

As the Maoist era CCP attacked "capitalist" practices and attitudes, Wenzhou's reputation as an outlaw prefecture grew. This identification was primarily associated with local economic practices that ran counter to socialist orthodoxy and central policy. While these practices can be seen as individual or household strategies for survival, self-help, or profit, they implicated the whole area in a network of nonlegal or underground production and trade that represented a challenge to the political and ideological control of the party-state.

In 1956, during a lull in the collectivization movement, one county in Wenzhou prefecture undertook China's first experiment with the household contract system in agriculture. This experiment spread throughout the prefecture, only to be singled out and harshly denounced at the central level during the subsequent antirightist campaign. In spite of central-level condemnation, peasant family farming was never completely eliminated in the area.[30]

During the Cultural Revolution, Wenzhou was designated as the archetype of the capitalist restoration (*ziben zhi bifu duanxing*) for its numerous unlicensed peddlers, black markets, smuggling, and underground workshops. Members of the "Cultural Revolution Leading Small Group" in Beijing reportedly found that "if you want to see capitalism in China, then you can just go to Wenzhou."[31] Replete with black markets and other forms of "speculation and profiteering" in the late 1960s and 1970s, Wenzhou, except at the height of the policing campaigns, made private economic activity an important aspect of the economy, even when it was not legal or licensed.[32]

In Yishan township in the southern part of the prefecture, for example, peasants took advantage of the factionalism and uncertainty of the Cultural Revolution to collect rags and reestablish the illegal cottage weaving industry that had been eliminated first with the imposition of a unified state purchase of cotton in 1952 and again in 1964 during the "four cleans" campaign, a precursor to the Cultural Revolution. Eliminated once again in the immediate aftermath of the Cultural Revolution in 1970, private household-based industry emerged once again in 1973 and was finally legalized in the 1980s.[33] This pattern of promoting household industry in the interstices of the system and in opposition to central policy was duplicated in much of the prefecture throughout the 1960s and 1970s, though the products and schemes varied.[34]

Underground activities were not limited to the countryside or to small market towns or to small commodity production and sale. In the larger county towns and in Wenzhou city proper (Lucheng), local people took up handicrafts, trade, and services and set up household industries.[35] These activities often were operated in a "half open" manner (ban gongkai). Black markets in timber and other materials also sprang up in the suburban areas of Wenzhou city. In the 1970s, the public sector stagnated and state organs lost the power to deal with the economy. In their place, underground shops and factories became quite active. In addition, there was underground production of vital materials and energy that were no longer being supplied by the state, as well as the development of a private system of transportation to replace facilities that had been paralyzed by the Cultural Revolution.[36]

For so much underground activity to exist and thrive, it required the cooperation of local officials. An approach taken by many local cadres in regulating private economic pursuits is described literally by some as "opening one eye and closing the other" (kaizhi yan bizhi yan). Some local leaders have maintained that they had no choice but to take up an attitude of deliberate indifference to the underground market known as bu-

*wen buwen*, or "don't ask, don't tell," also called "governance through nonaction" (*wuwei erzhi*).[37] Many cadres found that they too could benefit from the growth of the household sector, both from the increased revenues generated through fees and taxes (legal and extralegal) and by getting into business themselves. The successful operation of private enterprise in China at this time required an extensive "connections network" (*guanxi wang*). Local administrative elites opened "back doors" for the private entrepreneurs with whom they had established strong personal connections.

The chaos of the Cultural Revolution that facilitated the popular expansion of an underground economy also saw the resurrection of other popular traditions in Wenzhou, or what one observer called "the restoration of the old culture." During the lantern festival of 1968 in villages all over Wenzhou, the traditional dragon lanterns and parades returned on a larger scale than the area had seen in years. In addition, traditional plays, called "black plays" during the Cultural Revolution, were performed throughout this period, even though they were banned by the central state. There was even a 1976 performance of *Hai Rui Dismissed from Office* (*Hui rui diu guan*) in a mountain district of Youngjia county. The play dramatized the dismissal of an upright Ming dynasty official who had returned to the peasants land that had been taken unjustly by uncaring government officials. Interpreted as an Aesopian attack on Maoist policies, the play had been harshly criticized early in the Cultural Revolution but still found an audience in Youngjia county, far from the center of power. As with the underground economy, the revival of popular culture could have occurred only with the acquiescence, if not the outright cooperation, of local officials.[38]

Community cooperation in defiance of the national center did not eliminate divisions and cleavages within local society. Relations of patronage and exchange that made up the underground economy are potentially highly exploitative. Deep cleavages did exist in Wenzhou. Nevertheless, local people acted cooperatively to resist central control through the exercise of what James Scott refers to as "everyday forms of resistance" —that power exercised by the apparently passive and "powerless" peasants as they pursue their own, sometimes petty interests, outside of the formal and institutionalized political system.[39] The exercise of such everyday power in Wenzhou fed a sense of local distinctiveness. When Mao died and reformers in the late 1970s and 1980s implemented a new national policy of economic reform that rewarded market activities, the switch permitted a renegotiation of the identity of Wenzhou that would directly engage the question of national self definition. The outlaw was now a model. The traitor of socialism had become an example of a successfully expanding economy.

## The Wenzhou Model as a Positive Identity
### The Wenzhou Model

What became known in the 1980s as the "Wenzhou model" had developed well before the advent of Deng Xiaoping's reform effort. Elements of the model included (1) household industries, (2) private wage labor and a labor market, (3) commodity markets, and even (4) lending and banking arrangements. With the initiation of promarket reform at the central level, Wenzhou's prior underground economy could be gradually legalized. The economy grew and its structure changed dramatically.

By the mid-1980s the private sector outgrew its officially stated purpose of filling in gaps in the state and collective economy. By the end of 1985 state-owned industry in Wenzhou accounted for only 18 percent of industrial output, more than two-thirds below the national average. Collective industry made up 52 percent, and private or individual (including household) industry made up an unprecedented 30 percent of Wenzhou's industrial value.[40] These official numbers actually understate the output of the private sector because many private enterprises, especially large-scale firms, were licensed as collectives.[41] A nominal collective status continued to be preferred by many entrepreneurs because of both the political risks of going private and the tax benefits of being designated collective. The area was becoming famous for the number of "ten thousand yuan" households, referring to their huge annual incomes.

Wenzhou was lauded by supporters of reform both nationally and locally as a model for rural and small-town development that did not require any additional state investment. The *World Economic Reporter*, a bold proreform Shanghai paper, declared that the southern part of the prefecture was "so rich it bled oil."[42] More cautious supporters saw Wenzhou as a unique example of successful development, while others suggested that it was a model that could be replicated elsewhere. In 1986 the national center made Wenzhou a special experimental zone for the development of the commodity economy.

**Opposition to the Wenzhou Model**

Detractors of the Wenzhou model saw it as a threat to the political and ideological hegemony of the central state. They were concerned that Wenzhou represented not just the expansion of the private sector but an outright negation of socialism. They discussed Wenzhou as the rise of capitalism with its class-based exploitation.

Actually, Wenzhou made Beijing's socialism irrelevant, offering a channel for upward mobility outside the party-state. Such success made prominent alternative values and definitions of success and competence in direct conflict with official socialist orthodoxy. By the late 1980s some were questioning central officials whether Wenzhou was even under the control of the center.

While Wenzhou was increasingly associated in the public mind with business prowess, rapid development, and new wealth, Wenzhou people in the 1980s were condemned in the official press for swindling, conspicuous consumption, gambling, and a revial of "feudal" practices.[43] The growing number of expensive funerals and gravesites became a focus of national attention.[44] Thus, during the first decade of reform, Wenzhou became a symbol for the development of the market and the private economy that continued to be controversial, especially during periods when the center reimposed its controls through economic or political retrenchment.

# The New Wenzhou Narrative

The rise of Wenzhou as a symbol in the national debate over China's future was marked by a growing sense of local pride and the emergence of a new Wenzhou narrative that presented a positive historic account of local wealth, economic practices, and resistance to the center. In my interviews in Wenzhou in 1989, officials and entrepreneurs proudly pointed out the manifestations of new wealth: new and increasingly elaborate family housing, expensive clothing, and fashionable haircuts. They noted that this wealth was locally produced. Local independence from the center was clearly a point of pride, even among cadres in publicly run enterprises. Management cadres who worked in one of Wenzhou's largest public enterprises boasted that while they were not prepared to sell things on the street, they were no longer willing to depend on the state for their personal needs.[45] They described the new houses they had built for themselves, noting that they were in this way quite different from the people in Hangzhou or the rest of China who were satisfied to live in substandard state housing and depend on the state. Wenzhou was different—entrepreneurial, self-reliant, modern, successful.

Leninist party systems have generally tended to make people wards of the state by subsidizing and organizing the production and distribution of goods and services and by providing a very austere welfare system. Citizens are thus dependent on and controlled by a state that can deny jobs, housing, and other benefits. While the welfare system was less extensive in China than in Europe or the USSR, it did provide minimal cradle-to-grave benefits for most urban residents. Residents of urban Wenzhou city were independent of the state in this respect, even to the point of ridiculing those who continued to rely on the party-state. Still, while they were finding greater autonomy, given the continuing power of the centralized system, people in Wenzhou continued to live and work and negotiate their identity within the framework of the state socialist system and its official symbols.

### Redefining the Private as Public

The new local narrative sought to coopt official socialist language by repackaging private as public. Private ventures were labeled *cooperative.* The so-called shareholding cooperatives (*gufen hezuo qiye*) in Wenzhou have become one of the most dynamic areas of the economy. In most cases a small group of friends or relatives holds the majority of shares in the firm and operates it as a private enterprise called a cooperative. Many firms have undertaken the shareholding structure because it is politically less risky.[46]

At a more general level, local officials undertook an effort to "rectify names,"[47] whereby all private and quasi-private operations were renamed in a way that would be in keeping with socialist norms. Thus, household industries, private firms, shareholding cooperatives, and other hybrid forms were called "people-run" (*minying* or *minban*) firms, invoking Maoist traditions.[48]

The redefinition of private as public marked a new activism at the local level that attempted to identify private interest with the public good and public spiritedness. It demonstrated an attempt by entrepreneurs and cadres at the local level to gain control of the naming process and to reinterpret socialist symbols in their effort to define themselves as at one with the national good. What had been a geographically based group identity was now being preferred as the basis for a new ideologically justified identity. The rectification of names and the new uses of such terms as cooperative provided an interpretation that valued successful entrepreneurship and wealth. It involved the conscious cooptation of the state's language and legitimizing concepts in an effort to gain control of the production of "common sense" and, thereby, the definition of positive identity.[49] Supported by the *mutualism* of familial and kinship ties, this new identity rested on *competence* in household manufacturing, entrepreneurship, and trade (see chapters 2 and 4).

## Reclaiming Wenzhou History

Local cadres began to reexamine Wenzhou's past. While such efforts are necessarily circumscribed by the still-dominant central party-state policy and ideology, they represent an attempt to reclaim, rehabilitate, and celebrate Wenzhou's recent history. Thus, in a series of books on the Wenzhou model edited by Lin Bai, Jin Guowen, Zhou Yilin, and Hu Fangsong, all cadres associated with the *Wenzhou Daily*,[50] the account of the 1956 decollectivization of agriculture,[51] an episode that brought state imposed suffering for those involved, was reconceived as a source of both local and personal pride.

In a book entitled *Wenzhou's Cadres,* stories are told of Li Yunhe and other cadres who promoted local development even though their actions were, at the time they began, illegal or in opposition to central policy. They are now presented as competent and caring cadres, in tune with the needs and interests of the people.[52]

In *Wenzhou's Peasant Entrepreneurs,* rural entrepreneurs are celebrated for their business acumen and for the ways that their entrepreneurship, growing out of local conditions, persisted in the face of hardship and served local needs.[53] Often such entrepreneurs began by engaging in illegal activity in the Cultural Revolution, typically as marketing and purchasing agents. Others are praised for establishing "money houses," pawnshops, and other private banking and lending practices. The celebration of such activities is especially striking as a transformation of values, given the long association of usury and pawnshops with peasant exploitation before the revolution. Wenzhou narratives reassess previously denigrated activities and promote a new sense of local competence. Episodes from Wenzhou's past that were once evidence of local immorality and failure are retold so as to demonstrate the vitality, competence, and creativity of the local people and their leaders. Good local party-state officials are identified with Wenzhou in opposition to the central state or state socialism. The identity of nation and local are thus being renegotiated.

This new local narrative is informed by a powerful petty capitalist worldview and echoes the petty commodity capitalism that challenged the Confucian hegemony of late imperial China.[54] Constructed as an alternative to the bureaucratic worldview institutionalized in formal state socialist structures and practices, Wenzhou's way offers a channel of upward mobility based on wealth and outside the CCP. The new petty commodity economy of Wenzhou, and the local identity associated with it, is rooted in family-based economic practices and resonates with anti-state or at least anti-center sentiments.[55] This new vision sees the central government bureaucracy as irrelevant at best. As such the narrative not only creates a new vision of local initiative, dynamism, and solidarity but also fundamentally challenges the official state socialist interpretation of the Chinese national identity and with it the legitimacy of the central party-state.

## Wenzhou Identity and Emergent Class Interests

Local identity as it developed in the 1980s promoted newly emerging economic interests that both strengthened and subverted local solidarities. A new class of wealthy entrepreneurs emerged. It included not only former peasants and unemployed urban youth, who were originally encouraged to undertake individual economic activity, but also cadres, former cadres, and their families.[56] This strengthened local solidarity.

Income gaps between employees and their employers are significant and growing. While there have always been deep social divisions in Wenzhou, the basis for these divisions is changing and their visibility is growing. A survey of eighty-four private enterprises in Wenzhou found that the average annual income reported by owners was 35.6 times that of their employees' average annual wage.[57] A survey of private (*siying*) enterprises found that 46 percent of workers were not satisfied with their incomes or benefits;[58] and there are reports that in some rural areas where labor has been in short supply there have been instances of slowdowns and strikes.[59] The potential for conflict is not just between workers and owners but also between cultivators and noncultivators, and between those in market-based enterprises and those in state units. That is to say, between those who are best positioned to take advantage of the market and those who are not. While analysis of these divisive dynamics exists in the literature on Wenzhou, local cadre efforts to reinvent Wenzhou and reclaim its history have typically ignored them in favor of a focus on shared identity and interests.

The strength of market forces in Wenzhou remains constricted by the twists and turns in central policy. An effort in Wenzhou to organize a "people-run enterprise" association was largely unsuccessful. Founded in February 1989 to represent the interests of private and quasi-private enterprises, this organization all but stopped functioning in the wake of the Tiananmen massacre and the ensuing political crackdown.[60] Still, new material-based interests promoted by the continuation of economic reform are forming locally and nationally. An experience of exploitation that divides owners from workers in Wenzhou may be creating an angry group that would respond to populist antimarket rhetoric from antireform groups at the center. The future is quite contested.

# Conclusion: Local Group Identity and National Transformation

Communalist local place ties in China have historically been the basis for collective action in the form of merchant guilds and native place associations. Such local ties in Wenzhou were reinforced in the postrevolutionary period by harsh central policies and became the basis for local solidarity and resistance to the central party-state. Wenzhou people took advantage of the weakening of the party-state after the Cultural Revolution to pursue popular local interests and new and old forms of entrepreneurialism, further weakening national power.

What it meant to be a Wenzhou person changed fundamentally. Wenzhou's identity can be seen as the basis for instrumental action at the local level. It can also be seen as an act of collective imagination, an invention, and a symbol that was defined and redefined in the constant struggle. Cast as a negative identity by the party-state in the 1960s, Wenzhou was reimagined by local entrepreneurs and cadres as a positive, and even alternative, identity when central policy relaxed in the 1980s. Since Wenzhou competed to be a national model, its local identity could reshape national identity.

The renegotiation of Wenzhou's identity in the 1980s was part of what Friedman has called a new national narrative that challenges the political hegemony and legitimacy of the state socialist system. The new national project sees Chinese national identity shifting from the northern hinterland, associated with statism, authoritarianism, and bureaucracy, to the dynamic southern coastal region.[61] The southern vision of a new Chinese national identity is more heterogenous, more cosmopolitan, and more entrepreneurial than the vision emanating from the north, and it regards the Leninist regime as an obstacle to China's continuing development. The economic dynamism of the south in the 1980s was not experienced as the result of central policy but as the product of innovative and entrepreneurial local people.

When localism raises questions about the national identity, it necessarily tests central state authority and power. It can also undermine national unity. Communalist struggles over identity in Eastern Europe, Russia, and elsewhere make clear the weaknesses of national integration in a transitional period, especially where Leninism has destroyed prior bases for societal solidarity. Communalist identities based on real or imagined primordial ties are more emotionally compelling and therefore easier to embrace, even more so during periods of economic and political uncertainty. When communal identities become the sole basis for societal consciousness and monopolize the political arena, the prospects for peaceful, let alone democratic, reintegration seem increasingly slim. The question is, has the Wenzhou narrative been merely local, or has its success contributed to the renegotiation of national identity? The evidence presented here suggests that the implications of Wenzhou's local experience reached well beyond Wenzhou.

Wenzhou and the larger southern challenge to the ideological hegemony of the center does not necessarily portend the disintegration of China; certainly localism in Wenzhou has not become separatism. By presenting an alternative interpretation of the national identity, Wenzhou, and the southern coastal region more generally, creates a new basis for the integration of China. It is more pluralistic and dynamic, and it promotes the formation of class- or interest-based solidarities. These cross-cutting solidarities may allow for, although they certainly do not guarantee, the development of a more stable and potentially more democratic future.

THE POWER OF IDENTITY

## Acknowledgment

This chapter is based on research conducted in Zhejiang Province, China, in 1986, 1989, and 1993. An earlier version of this chapter was prepared for presentation at the symposium on Chinese Identities sponsored by the Center for Chinese Studies, University of California, Berkeley, 25–26 February 1994.

## Notes

1. Yu Naiyun, "Guanyu Wenzhou jingji gaige yu jiefan sixiang de sikao" (Concerning the Wenzhou's Economic Reform and the Liberation of Thought), *Zhejiang Xuekan* 5 (1992).

2. For an overview of the concept, see Philip Gleason, "Identity: A Semantic History," *Journal of American History* 69 (1983): 910–31, and the preceding chapters in this book. On China, see Lowell Dittmer and Samuel Kim, "In Search of a Theory of National Identity," in *China's Quest for National Identity*, ed. Lowell Dittmer and Samuel Kim (Ithaca, N.Y.: Cornell University Press, 1993).

3. Perry Link, *Evening Chats in Beijing: Probing China's Predicament* (New York: Norton, 1992), 175.

4. For an analysis of these three approaches to ethnic identity, see Crawford Young, "The Dialectics of Cultural Pluralism," in *The Rising Tide of Cultural Pluralism: The Nation-State at Bay*, ed. Crawford Young (Madison: University of Wisconsin Press, 1993).

5. See Dittmer and Kim, "In Search of a Theory," 27–30, on the difference between a crisis of inclusion and the crisis of self-definition in national identity.

6. Ernest Gellner, *Nations and Nationalism* (Ithaca, N.Y.: Cornell University Press, 1983).

7. See, for example, Marie-Claire Bergere, "The Shanghai Bankers' Association, 1915–1927: Modernization and the Institutionalization of Local Solidarities"; and Bryna Goodman, "New Culture, Old Habits"; both in *Shanghai Sojourners*, ed. Frederic Wakeman Jr. and Wen-Hsin Yeh (Berkeley: University of California Press, 1992).

8. Myron Cohen, "Being Chinese: The Peripheralization of Traditional Identity," *Daedalus*, Spring 1991, 121.

9. James Watson, "Rites or Beliefs? The Construction of a Unified Culture in Late Imperial China," in Dittmer and Kim, *China's Quest*.

10. Ibid.

11. See, for example, Audrey Donnithome and Nicholas Lardy, "Centralization and Decentralization in China's Fiscal Management," *China Quarterly* 68 (June 1976):328–54; Vivienne Shue, *The Reach of the State: Sketches of the Body Politic* (Stanford: Stanford University

Press, 1988); Helen Sui, *Agents and Victims in South China: Accomplices in Rural Revolution* (New Haven: Yale University Press, 1989).

12. John P. Burns, *The Chinese Communist Party's Nomenklatura System* (New York: M.E. Sharpe, 1989).

13. Suisheng Zhao, "From Coercion to Negotiation: The Changing Central-Local Economic Relationship in Mainland China," *Issues & Studies* 28 (October 1992):1–22.

14. Edward Friedman, "The Politics of Local Models, Social Transformation and Power Struggles in the People's Republic of China: Tachai and Teng Hsiao-p'ing," *China Quarterly* 76 (December 1978): 823–90.

15. This discussion of Wenzhou draws from Kristen Parris, "Local Society and the State: The Wenzhou Model and the Making of Private Sector Policy" (Ph.D. dissertation, Indiana University, 1991). See also Kristen Parris, "Local Initiative and National Reform: The Wenzhou Model of Development," *China Quarterly* 134 (June 1993):242–63.

16. For historical background on Wenzhou and Zhejiang Province, see Mary Rankin, *Elite Activism and Political Transformation in China: Zhejiang Province 1865–1911* (Stanford: Stanford University Press, 1986).

17. There is a minority *she* population of approximately 50,000 located mostly in Pingyang, Cangnan, Taixun, and Ruian counties in the southern part of the prefect.

18. Yuan Enzhen, *Wenzhou moshi yu fu yu zhilu* (Wenzhou Model of Economy and the Road to Affluence) (Shanghai: Shanghai shehui kexue yuan chubanshe, 1987), 9.

19. Sun Rudong, "Zou nan chuang bei de Wenzhou ren" (Wenzhou people going south and charging north), *Dangdai renkou* (Contemporary population) 1, 1992.

20. It should be noted that in spite of their self-perceived role as bridges, Wenzhou people can be quite closed regarding contacts with outsiders. A representative of the New York Wenzhou Hometown Association told me that the only reason he was willing to see me was because a friend from Wenzhou, who spoke the dialect, had arranged the meeting, accompanied me to the meeting, and interpreted for me.

21. Lynn White and Li Cheng, "China Coast Identities: Regional, National, Global," in Dittmer and Kim, *China's Quest*, 162–63.

22. On local Chinese languages and dialects, see John DeFrancis, *The Chinese Language: Fact and Fantasy* (Honolulu: University of Hawaii Press, 1984), 53–67.

23. Y. Ding, "Some suggestions on the problem of the standardization of Chinese language," in *Xiandai hanyu guifan wenti xueshu huiyi wenjian huibien,* cited in Alan P.I. Liu, "The Politics of Corruption in the People's Republic of China," *American Political Science Review* 77 (1983):614.

24. This story was told by several people during formal interviews and informal conversations with the author. I have no independent verification of its validity, but even if it is not true, it demonstrates the importance of the local language and sense of local distinctiveness.

25. On local identity as a basis for prejudice, see Emily Honig, "Invisible Inequalities: The Status of Subei People in Contemporary Shanghai," *China Quarterly*, June 1990, 272–92; and Antonia Finnane, "The Origins of Prejudice: The Malintegration of Subei in the Late Imperial China," *Comparative Studies in Social and History* 35 (April 1992):211–316.

26. Ya-Ling Liu, "The Private Economy and Local Politics in Wenzhou," *China Quarterly* 130 (June 1992):293–316.

27. Between 1949 and 1981, total state investment in Wenzhou amounted to 655 million yuan, while investment in Ningbo was 2.8 billion. According to official statistics, Wenzhou experienced an industrial growth rate of only 0.1 percent between 1966 and 1978. This figure does not include activity of the underground economy, which was very active at this time, but it does indicate the failure of the public economy to grow and meet local needs. Ma Jinlong, "An Introduction to Wenzhou's Economic Situation," in *Youguan wenzhou jingji de bufen zhongyao jianghua* (Some Important Talks Regarding Wenzhou's Economy), a special issue of *Jiaoyan ziliao* (Teaching and Research materials), 1 July 1986.

28. Kenneth Hoover, "Identity and Democratization," a paper prepared for the Research Committee on Political Philosophy, World Congress of the International Political Science Association, Berlin, August 1994, 10–12. See also chap. 5 above.

29. Lynn T. White, *Policies of Chaos: The Organizational Causes of Violence in China's Cultural Revolution* (Princeton: Princeton University Press, 1989), 8.

30. For accounts of this episode, see *Zhejiang hezuohua shi liao* (Materials on Cooperativization History in Zhejiang) 3 (11 October 1988), entire issue; Zhang Jun, "Yu wushengchu ting jing lei— zhongguo nongcun gaige jishi" (Listening to Frightening Thunder from an Obscure Place—A Chronology of China's Rural Reform), *Zixue* (Self Study) 2 (1988):10–17; Li Yunhe, "Nongcun 'huxue' chutan" (Initial Investigation of Rural "Householdology"), *Zhejiang xuekan* (Zhejiang Studies) 1 (1985):17–23; and *Renmin ribao* (People's Daily), 12 October 1984, 2.

31. Zhu Youdi and Chen Shengfa, *Wenzhou baofa* (Wenzhou Nouveau Riche) (Guilin: Lijiang chubanshe, 1989), 35.

32. Yu Binghui, ""Zhengzhi, jingji, shehui: dui Wenzhou moshi de zaikaochao" (Politics, Economy, Society: A Reconsideration of the Wenzhou Model), *Nongcun Jingji yu shehu* (Rural Economics and Society), 2 (1988):13–14.

33. Li Jianguang, Li Guo, and Tan Hong, "Wenzhou jingji de fazhan: yizhong suoyouquan lilun de chanshi" (Wenzhou Economic Development: An Explication of the Property Theory), manuscript, 1988, 24.

34. "Shangouli de 'dongfang di yi niukou shichang'" (The "Orient's Number One Button Market" Situated in a Gully), in *Wenzhou de shichang* (Wenzhou Markets), ed. Lin Bai, Jin Guowen, Zhou Penglin, and Hu Fangsong (Guilin: Renmin Chubanshe, 1987), 65.

35. Parris, "Local Society,"; Yu Binghui, "Politics," 10.

36. Yu Binghui, "Politics," 13–14.

37. Lu Shengliang, "Minban gongye de fazhan gei Wenzhou chengxiang cengtian de shengji" (People-Run Industry Gives Rural and Urban Wenzhou Added Vitality), in *Wenzhou nongcun shangpin jingji xin geju* (The New Pattern of Wenzhou's Rural Commodity Economy) (Wenzhou: n.p., December 1985).

38. Yu Binghui, "Politics," 12.

39. James Scott, *The Weapons of the Weak: Everyday Forms of Peasant Resistance* (New Haven: Yale University Press, 1985).

40. Dong Chaocai, "Xingshi yu gaige" (Trends and reform), in *Yanjiu ziliao* (Research Materials), 28 July 1986, 45.

41. In 1988, for example, when shareholding firms were included, the private sector reportedly accounted for 59 percent of total industrial output value. Zhejiang Private Economy Research Group, "A Special Report Regarding the Internal Relations in the Private Economy," manuscript, May 1990, 8.

42. *Shijie jingii daobao* (World Economic Reporter), 13 February 1984, 8.

43. See examples in *Zhenan Nan RiBao* (South Zhejiang Daily), 4 April 1983.

44. See reports in *Shijie jingji baodao*, 30 January and 13 February 1984. These expenditures were obvious to any visitor.

45. Personal conversations with the author.

46. On shareholding enterprises, see Zhejiang Province, "Wenzhou gufen hezuo qiye tizhi yanjiu" (Wenzhou Shareholding Cooperative Enterprise System Research), *Wenzhou shichan jingji yu gufen hezuo qiye* (Wenzhou Market Economy and Shareholding Cooperative Enterprises), published by *Wenzhou luntan*, 1993.

47. This Confucian term refers to the need for names (i.e., concepts) to reflect their correct nature and function in society, in accordance with the correct principles of the universe.

48. This term begins to appear in the local newspaper in early 1983. See *Zhenan ribao* (South Zhejiang Daily), 29 March 1983, for the first headline using this expression; see also Lu Shenliang, "Minban gongye."

49. For other attempts to coopt or subvert the dominant discourse,

see James Scott, *Domination and the Arts of Resistance* (New Haven: Yale University Press, 1990), 102.

50. Lin Bai et al., *Wenzhou Moshi congshu* (Nanning: Guangxi Chubanshe, 1987).

51. Lin Bai et al., "Baochan daohu zhangdaozhe—ji Li Yunhe" (Initiator of Household Contracting—Remembering Li Yunhe), in Lin Bai et al., *Wenzhou de Ganbu* (Nanning: Guangxi Renmin Chubanshe, 1987), 79–78.

52. Lin Bai et al., *Wenzhou de ganbu*, 69–78.

53. Lin Bai et al., *Wenzhou de nongmin qiyejia* (Wenzhou's Peasant Entrepreneurs) (Nanning: Guangxi Renmin Chubanshe, 1987).

54. Hill Gates, "Money for the Gods," *Modern China* 13 (July 1987):261.

55. Ibid., 263.

56. It is important to note that the term "cadres" has a very broad meaning in China, referring not just to party state officials but also to civil servants and teachers. See Ole Oldgaard, "Entrepreneurs and Elite Formation in Rural China," *Australian Journal of Chinese Affairs* 28 (July 1992):89–108.

57. Zhejiang Private Economy Research Small Group, "A Special Report," 5. Gaps in incomes were reported to be much higher in Hebei and Guangdong.

58. Zhejiang Private Enterprise Economy Research Group, "Ten Proposals Regarding the Development of Our Province's Private Enterprise Economy," manuscript, May 1990, 4.

59. Xu Hongzhuan and Tai Huijun, "A Survey and Analysis of Wenzhou's Private Enterprise Labor System," *Yanhai jingii* (Coastal Economy) 4 (1991):14.

60. Personal communication with participants.

61. Edward Friedman, "China's North-South Split and the Forces of Disintegration," *Current History*, September 1993; and Edward Friedman, "Reconstructing China's National Identity: A Southern Alternative to Mao-Era Anti-Imperialist Nationalism," *Journal of Asian Studies* 53 (February 1994):67–91.

# APPENDIX

## Organ-Mode Stages

| Organ-Mode Stages | | 1 | 2 | 3 |
|---|---|---|---|---|
| Maturity | VIII | | | |
| Adulthood | VII | | | |
| Young adulthood | VI | | | |
| Puberty and adolescence | V | Temporal perspective vs. Time confusion | Self-certainty vs. Self-consciousness | Role experimentation vs. Role fixation |
| Latency | IV | | | |
| Locomotor-genital | III | | | INITIATIVE vs. GUILT |
| Muscular-anal | II | | AUTONOMY vs. SHAME, DOUBT | |
| Oral-sensory | I | TRUST vs. MISTRUST | | |

Phases

NOTE: The basic chart appears in Erik H. Erikson, *Identity: Youth and Crisis* (New York: Norton, 1968), 94, and is reprinted by permission of W.W. Norton and Company. In a version printed in Kenneth Hoover, *A Politics of Identity: Liberation and the Natural Community* (Urbana: University of Illinois Press, 1975), 114, I added the labels (*Maturity*, etc.) given to the

OF EPIGENETIC HUMAN DEVELOPMENT

| 4 | 5 | 6 | 7 | 8 |
|---|---|---|---|---|
| | | | | INTEGRITY vs. DESPAIR |
| | | | GENERATIVITY vs. STAGNATION | |
| | | INTIMACY vs. ISOLATION | | |
| Apprenticeship vs. Work paralysis | IDENTITY vs. IDENTITY CONFUSION | Sexual polarization vs. Bisexual confusion | Leader- and followership vs. Authority confusion | Ideological commitment vs. Confusion of values |
| INDUSTRY vs. INFERIORITY | Task identification vs. Sense of futility | | | |
| | Anticipation of roles vs. Role inhibition | | | |
| | Will to be oneself vs. Self-doubt | | | |
| | Mutual recognition vs. Autistic isolation | | | |

*of Cultural Response*

"Organ-Mode Stages" by Erikson in a less complete form of the chart appearing in Erik H. Erikson, *Childhood and Society* (New York: Norton, 1950, 1963), 273. The titles "Organ-Mode Stages" and "Phases of Cultural Response" have also been added by me.

# Index

# About the Authors

Kenneth Hoover is professor of political science at Western Washington University, where he became chair of the department in 1988. Earlier, he taught for ten years at the University of Wisconsin-Parkside, where he won the Distinguished Teaching Award, and for eight years at the College of Wooster. While completing his Ph.D. with Prof. Murray Edelman at the University of Wisconsin-Madison, he taught at the University of Wisconsin-Whitewater.

Hoover is the author of five books on political theory, ideology, and methodology. His recent works deal with contemporary political forces: *Ideology and Political Life,* 2d ed. (1994), and *Conservative Capitalism in Britain and the United States: A Critical Perspective* (1988) with Raymond Plant, Master of St. Catherine's College, Oxford. *The Elements of Social Scientific Thinking* (1995), 6th ed., with Todd Donovan, is widely used as a framework for understanding the social sciences.

James Marcia is professor of psychology at Simon Fraser University in Vancouver, B.C. Since finishing his Ph.D. at Ohio State University, he has become a leading international expert on the social psychology of identity.

Kristen Parris is associate professor of political science at Western Washington University. The author of several articles on Chinese politics, she received her Ph.D. from Indiana University.